God Is
in the
Kitchen
Too

P. B. WILSON

HARVEST HOUSE™ PUBLISHERS

EUGENE, OREGON

Cover by Koechel Peterson & Associates, Inc., Minneapolis, Minnesota

GOD IS IN THE KITCHEN TOO
Copyright © 2003 by P.B. Wilson
Published by Harvest House Publishers
Eugene, Oregon 97402

Library of Congress Cataloging-in-Publication Data

Wilson, P. B. (P. Bunny), 1950-
    God is in the kitchen too / P.B. Wilson.
        p. cm—(Are you looking for God?)
ISBN 0-7369-0795-5 (pbk.)
1. Christian women—Religious life.   2. Cookery—Religious aspects—Christianity.
I. Title.   II. Series.
    BV4527 .W556 2003
    248.8'43—dc21   2002153425

Printed in the United States of America.

03 04 05 06 07 08 09 10 11 / ML-MS / 10 9 8 7 6 5 4 3 2 1

Contents

To my Mentoring Fellowship women—
Isaiah 26:3

~

Acknowledgments

Thus far, this has been my most difficult book to write. Physical challenges slowed me down greatly, and at one point two friends had to step in to help me. They sat at the computer and typed as I dictated to them. Thank you Karen Bradford and Helen Franklin.

Also, it is with great appreciation that I thank Mary Dumas and Sandy Snavely for giving me their input on this book. How I treasure our friendship and the many hours you have invested in reading my material.

I want to thank my publisher, Harvest House, and especially Betty Fletcher and Barbara Gordon. You overextended yourself to make this book a reality, and I am grateful for all your hard work.

Finally, I want to thank my husband, Frank. We were married 20 years before I understood that cooking was a ministry. Prior to that I tried to do as little of it as possible, and I know at times that was frustrating for you. Your patience has allowed me to grow into the wife and mother God desires for me to be.

1
It's Time

~

O kay, ladies, it's time for us to dig in. No more fooling around; this is serious business! We've been laughed at, ridiculed and run out of one of the most important rooms in our homes. It is a God-designed refuge filled with untold spiritual pleasures and purpose. Since you read the title of this book you know I'm referring to the kitchen. "The kitchen!" some might exclaim. "You must be joking."

For years I avoided the kitchen at all cost. It seemed like a waste of time to be there because I had so many significant things to do. There were people to meet, projects to address and goals to be accomplished. But one day I uncovered the true value of my kitchen, and it has set me free. Free to taste God's goodness, to smell the aroma of His love and to see His perfect plan revealed.

Is this a book about cooking? Yes, but even more so, it is a book about spiritual maturity. Whether you are married, married with children or single, we are about to embark on a great adventure together, discovering God's love for the kitchen. Why? Because it is the place where we, as women of all shapes, sizes and walks of life, are able to bless family, friends and loved ones with delicious food and warm, tasty fellowship.

> *We've been laughed at, ridiculed and run out of one of the most important rooms in our homes.*

So are you ready? "Ready for what?" you might ask. Ready to experience the spiritual power and purpose locked away in your kitchen! Ready to discover the relaxation and renewal that awaits every participant. Ready to delight in the many spiritual victories that are yours when you understand God's design for your kitchen.

Are you wondering, "What in the world does this have to do with cooking?" The answer is, "Everything!"

It seems as if most women fall into one of these categories:

You love to cook but have paid little attention to its spiritual implications.

You know how to cook but would rather be doing something else.

You would like to know how to cook but you don't know where to begin.

Going into the kitchen completely intimidates you.

You hate cooking!

Feel free to add your category to the list. By the time you finish this book, my goal is to impart to you a love for cooking and an understanding of the spiritual power that awaits you when you grab hold of this nearly lost art. I want you to grasp the *why* of cooking not just the *how*.

Not for Me

Frank and I were married in 1973, and for the first 20 years of my marriage, I'd tell him from time to time that cooking was not my calling. I didn't "get" cooking. It takes you up to an hour to prepare it, an hour to clean it up and about half that time to eat it. I had a time management problem with cooking. The thought would often come to my mind, "Cereal, now who said that was a breakfast food? It seems to me that it works well anytime of the day!"

When my older children returned home from school they would often say, "Dad, what's for dinner?" They knew better than to ask me because it usually hadn't crossed my mind, and cooking was one of Frank's favorite pastimes. I was frustrated whenever I went into the kitchen because I immediately felt distracted from my list of "more important things" to do with my day. When I did cook, my level of concentration went on overload—how to get all that food on the table at the same time seemed impossible. *Help!*

Well, I was deceived by my own misconceptions. I was robbed blind of the many blessings that flow from the kitchen. My family was also being deprived of the rich experiences that take place around the dining room table. The conversations, laughter and fellowship were snuffed out in the midst of my busy schedule. But I thank God that my eyes were opened in time to correct my mistake, and He has been ever so gracious enough to redeem the time that was lost. I look forward to sharing more about that later in this book.

> *I* didn't understand—and no one ever told me—the great significance of cooking.

I didn't understand—and no one ever told me—the great significance of cooking. Therefore, I had no desire to learn or to pass it on to my children. In a world of fast food, free pizza delivery and frozen foods that can go straight from the freezer to the microwave, I felt relieved of any kitchen responsibility. But I was missing the point and had no idea of the fulfillment and satisfaction that awaited me.

Oh, we have so much to talk about—but I think we need a recipe break! How about something delightful to drink? If you're at home and have the ingredients, let's go into the kitchen and prepare a beverage. It is so relaxing to sip on something delicious.

Sip and Serve

When people visit our home, the first thing we should ask after they have taken a seat is, "Would you like something to drink?" This expression of thoughtfulness blesses the guests. And when special time and consideration has gone into preparing a thirst-quenching treat, it ministers to their minds, bodies and souls.

I have found that hospitality can be easily extended no matter what the weather may bring. A hot cup of tea warms the chill and a cold glass of lemonade cools the heat. Either way I've got you covered. The following are recipes for both drinks.

RECIPE   HOT GINGER TEA

1 cup (c.) of water
1 tea bag—Sweet Dreams Tea by Bigelow
Clover honey to taste
Ground ginger to taste

Bring water to a boil, pour over tea bag in cup and allow to steep (that means the bag sits in the water) for 3 minutes. Add honey to your liking, and shake in ground ginger a little at a time until you like the taste.

You can also make a decorator teapot full of tea. For every 1½ cups of water add a tea bag and follow the above directions. Allow it to steep for at least 5 minutes.

Hint: Adding a small plate of pastry, fresh fruit or some other type of snack is a wonderful addition.

COLD LEMONADE

1 gallon pitcher
1 ½ c. fresh lemon juice (about 6 to 7 lemons)
2 ½ c. Sugar in the Raw (or your preference of sugar)

Add sugar to pitcher. Cover sugar with water about 1" above sugar level. (Bottled or filtered water is best.) Stir. Let sit until dissolved, stirring occasionally. Add lemon juice, and then fill pitcher with water. Stir and refrigerate.

That was a refreshing break! Throughout this book, I will be sharing recipes that were not created by me. I learned to cook by watching other people with a notebook in my hand. I wrote down every single thing they did. The result is that today many of my friends and family say I am a fabulous cook—but that is only because I gleaned my recipes from other fabulous cooks. The recipes included in this book are designed to help women who don't know how to cook or are intimidated by the kitchen. So for those of you who read recipe books like a newspaper, it may seem as if I am going through a lot of unnecessary steps, but to the women who are fearful or feel completely inadequate in the kitchen, the extra effort will be a welcome relief. To keep the recipes easy to use, I include instructions for "beginners" and for "advanced" cooks.

Beginners, if you do not know how to cook, the grocery store may seem like an alien planet. Purchasing ingredients for a recipe can be frustrating because you may not know where to look. My suggestion is that you make up a list and ask one of the men or women who bag groceries to help you find the supplies. Most stores train their employees to be accommodating. I will be sharing the name brands I use in my recipes for your convenience.

Note: Before you begin cooking, run a sink full of hot soapy water so you can wash the dishes as you go along. When I serve dinner, the only dishes left to wash are the ones on the table and the pots on the stove.

I Can Do That!

Danielle (not her real name) was one of 18 women I mentored for a year. These married ladies came to my home once a month, and I taught them how to "love their husbands, to love their children, [to be] keepers at home" (Titus 2:4-5 KJV). The mentoring fellowship began at 6:30 P.M. with appetizers and was followed by a cooking lesson and Bible study. It concluded with us enjoying the delicious meal we prepared.

Danielle was married two-and-a-half years when she first attended the mentoring fellowship. She was completely intimidated by the kitchen because she wasn't allowed in that room when she was growing up. As a child, Angelique was very tiny and left-handed. Everyone else in her family was right-handed, so teaching her to cut and stir was awkward. Because of her slight frame, it was difficult for her to reach things. As she got older, Angelique lost all desire to enter or participate in activities connected to the kitchen. At some point in her life, she developed a fear of failure and felt she would be embarrassed if she even tried to cook. So she withdrew from any attempt except for one dish—spaghetti.

In the first class she attended, I showed her how to fry chicken and fish, as well as a few accompanying side dishes.

She stood in amazement at the simplicity. As the chicken was being removed from the skillet, she announced, "Is that all it takes? I can do that! I'm going to fix this for my husband tomorrow, but I'm going to make him leave the house because if he is there I will be totally intimidated."

Danielle's husband called the next evening to tell me that the fried chicken was "off the hook" (the younger generation's "fabulous")! Danielle, along with many other women I have met or mentored who were intimidated by the kitchen, inspired me to simplify the recipes included in this book. Just in case you haven't planned your dinner for tonight, let me share my fried chicken* with you.

The recipe instructions in this book are broken into two sections—beginners and advanced. If you are an experienced cook, the advanced sections give you the instructions minus the fine details.

FRIED CHICKEN

1 package (pkg.) fresh chicken pieces
salt
pepper
2 c. Gold Medal All-purpose Flour
vegetable or corn oil

Preparation time: 15 min.
Cooking time: 30 min.

Beginners

Select fresh chicken that is yellow in color. Some chickens are white, and that usually means they are old. If breasts are your favorite part, cut them in half for more complete cooking. (In the housewares section of the market they

---

* I'll be the first to admit that fried foods should be eaten in moderation, but every now and then they are a welcomed delight. There are other recipes in this book that are low in fat, and I'm looking forward to sharing them with you as well.

usually sell meat scissors. This will enable you to cut the chicken easily.)

The key to great fried chicken is that the vegetable or corn oil in the skillet is very hot and the chicken is turned only once.

Wear rubber gloves for two reasons: 1) they protect your hands from coming into contact with salmonella bacteria* sometimes found in chicken, and 2) they keep your hands and arms from being burned by hot, popping grease.

Run water over each chicken piece to clean it. Lay the chicken out and season it with salt and pepper. An even layer of seasoning across each piece is fine. (After you have tasted the finished product for the first time, you can then determine whether you want more or less seasoning the next time.) *Note:* chicken wings are in sections—the tip, middle and drumstick-looking part (drumette). Put the tip of the wing behind the part that looks like the drumstick, and you'll be able to get more in the skillet.

Pour the flour into a small paper bag and add 4 to 5 pieces of chicken, and then shake until they're evenly covered. Continue this process until all the chicken is floured.

Fill the skillet halfway with cooking oil and put the flame on high. (A cast iron skillet is best and can be purchased at a kitchen supply store—but don't wait until you have one to try this recipe.) The oil should be high enough to cover half the chicken. You can test the heat of the oil by dropping a small piece of chicken in the skillet. It should sizzle right away. Add the chicken a piece at a time, one right after the other. When the skillet is full, you will notice that the oil quickly cools down. It will once again get hot, and during this time the chicken is cooking on the inside.

---

* Because of the possibility of salmonella bacteria, I wash my hands very well with soap and warm water. I also clean off the areas the raw chicken has been in contact with (sink, cutting board and counter), using soap and Clorox bleach.

Wait until the chicken is golden brown on one side before turning (approximately 15 to 20 minutes). I suggest you use tongs to turn the chicken so you are not too close to the hot grease. Once the chicken is turned, it will fry in half the time as the first side. When done, put paper towels (two sheets folded) on a plate and place the chicken on the towels to drain the excess oil.

Advanced

Season chicken with salt and pepper. Flour chicken. Corn or vegetable oil should come halfway up the chicken in skillet (cast iron preferable). Oil should be very hot. Turn the chicken when it is brown, and turn only once.

FRIED FISH

Fresh fish (red snapper,
    filet of catfish, bass or trout)
salt
pepper
Albers yellow corn meal
vegetable or corn oil

Preparation time: 10 min.
Cooking time: 10 to 15 min.

Beginners

Purchase your fish at the fresh fish counter in the market. If it is a whole fish, ask them to remove the head, slice the fish in half and cut in 2" pieces. I usually buy extra fish so I can freeze some for future use.*

---

* *Freezing fish:* Put fresh fish in freezer bag (make sure to write the contents, quantity and date on the outside of the bag). Cover the fish with purified or bottled water and freeze. The water keeps the fish from freezer burn, and when you thaw it out it tastes as fresh as it did when you bought it.

Follow the directions for fried chicken. Since the fish are thin in depth, you'll use less oil. Still, the oil in the skillet should come halfway up the depth of the fish so that when you turn it over it will cook evenly on the second side. Fish fries quickly (5 to 10 minutes). It is important to fill the skillet quickly when adding the fish so that the oil will cool down. Wait until golden brown on one side before turning, and turn only once. If the fish is dry on the inside, then you know to cook it less the next time you prepare it.

Advanced

Follow directions for making fried chicken. The oil should be only half the depth of the fish.

The day I called Danielle for her approval to write this story in my book, she shared the tremendous blessing cooking has been in her life and that of her family. And she also shared a recipe with me for an appetizer she was going to make for an upcoming social gathering at her home! Danielle had also decided to make a peach cobbler to take to a picnic the following week. (The cobbler was the first dessert she learned to make at the mentoring fellowship.) Today she loves to cook because she discovered how easy it is, and she loves the joy delicious meals bring to those she serves.

I can do that! I'm going to fix this for my husband tomorrow...."

Perhaps you're one of those women who are intimidated by the kitchen, and even the extra explanations for the recipes failed to alleviate your apprehension. Let me suggest that you learn how to cook as I did. Do you know someone who is a great cook? What is your favorite dish he or she prepares? Ask the cook if you can purchase the ingredients and watch the dish being prepared. Many people love to fellowship with someone as they share their recipes. The key for beginners is to write down absolutely everything the cook does—the height of the flame, the approximate cooking time from one thing to another, the amount of seasoning used. (There are some blank recipe pages included at the end of this book for your convenience.)

Many times a person who is comfortable in the kitchen does not use measurements, so you have to develop your own measuring system. Also, when appropriate, sample the food as it is cooking so you can get an idea of what it should taste like as it proceeds to completion. One of the greatest keys, however, is to prepare that recipe within the next couple of days while it is still fresh in your mind. Let me also suggest that if your husband loves his mother's cooking, one of the greatest ways to bless him is to learn how to prepare some of his favorite dishes. Start hanging out in his mom's kitchen, pick up some valuable tips and then watch your husband's positive reaction.

As I mentioned earlier, I have never created a recipe, so I don't know what it feels like to be asked to divulge one of my creations. It is easy for me to pass on what has been so generously shared with me. If you have been given the gift of developing tasty cuisine, let me encourage you to share the recipes with others. I know some people who refuse to share their recipes. Maybe they need to be reminded that Philippians 2:4 says, "Do nothing out of selfish ambition or vain conceit, but in humility consider others better than yourselves." Sometimes our value is determined by the praise received from a dish we have prepared, and people may be waiting at the potluck table for you to arrive. Just think of the *greater* number of people you could bless if you spread that recipe around. Don't worry, every time it is prepared that family will remember it was you who blessed them. There are times when a recipe is kept secret because it will be used in a business venture or you made a promise to the person who taught you never to share it. That promise should be kept. I encourage those of you who can share to spread the wealth around.

Finishing the Meal

Let's add two side dishes to the chicken or fish by preparing rice and cabbage.

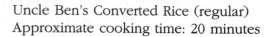 **RICE**

Uncle Ben's Converted Rice (regular)
Approximate cooking time: 20 minutes

Beginners and Advanced
Follow directions on the box for the desired number of people you are cooking for.

CABBAGE

1 large (lg.) head of cabbage
1 medium (med.) onion
1 smoked turkey leg
½ c. vegetable or corn oil
⅛ c. vegetable or corn oil
⅛ c. water
salt
pepper
raw sugar (Sugar in the Raw) or white sugar

Preparation time: 5 min.
Cooking time: 20 min.

Beginners
Ask the produce person how to select a good head of cabbage. (It should be firm when squeezed.)

Remove the top layer of leaves and wash by running under cold water.

Cut cabbage in half. There is a solid white core at the bottom of the cabbage in the center. Cut out that white core.

Place the cabbage on a cutting board with the flat side down. With a sharp knife (watch your fingers), slice into ½-inch strips and place in bowl.

Peel and slice medium onion into ¼" pieces.

Pour ½ c. of oil into skillet. Cut smoked turkey in slices off the bone and fry (braise) with a medium flame. Remove the turkey and put onions into the skillet. Cover and stir frequently until light brown.

In a pot large enough to hold the cut cabbage, add ⅛ c. cooking oil and heat under medium flame. Add cut cabbage to the pot along with ⅛ c. of water. Add smoked turkey and onions. Sprinkle salt, pepper and sugar across the top. Cover with lid. Stir every five minutes, using a big spoon to bring the cabbage at the bottom of the pot to the top. After cooking for 15 minutes, taste a piece. Determine if you need more spices. Cook to the desired texture (some people like it softer than others).

Preparation time for the chicken, rice and cabbage is approximately 20 minutes, so you can complete this meal in under an hour. Nice additions to the meal are corn bread and peach cobbler for dessert.

CORN BREAD

1 box Jiffy Corn Bread
1 teaspoon (tsp.) Sugar in the Raw
¼ c. melted butter
1 egg
¼ c. milk

Preheat oven to 400 degrees (*Note:* Whenever the recipe calls for the oven to be preheated, it is best to turn it on at least 15 minutes before inserting the dish into the oven.)
Preparation time: 5 min.
Baking time: 15 to 20 min.

Beginners and Advanced

Pour 1 tsp. of cooking oil into a cake pan or 8" pan. Spread the oil around the pan by using a small piece of Saran wrap or wax paper.

Pour the Jiffy mix into a bowl, along with the other ingredients and stir until blended well. Pour mixture into pan and put in the oven on the middle rack. Bake until golden brown (approximately 15 to 20 minutes).

Note: Heat rises to the top. If food is put on the top rack it bakes faster, and on the bottom rack food bakes slower.

You will be delighted with the following dessert because it is easy and soooooooo delicious!

 **PEACH COBBLER**

2 lg. cans Del Monte *Lite* sliced peaches
1 tablespoon (tbsp.) cinnamon
1 teaspoon (tsp.) nutmeg
3 tbsp. flour
1 ½ c. light brown sugar
1 tbsp. lemon juice
1 package (pkg.) regular Pillsbury
    Pet-Ritz Pie Crusts
1 stick regular butter (not unsalted butter
    or margarine)

Preheat oven: 400 degrees
Preparation time: 10 min.
Baking time: 50 to 60 min.

Beginners

Pillsbury Pet-Ritz Pie Crusts (frozen) is the best for this recipe. (If your grocery market doesn't carry it, ask them to order it. In the meantime, use another brand.) There are two piecrust shells in each package. Open the package and separate the piecrusts so they can slightly defrost while you are preparing the other ingredients.

In a large bowl add all the ingredients, except butter, and stir well. The flour will not dissolve completely, and it will make small white lumps. These will blend in during the baking.

Pour mixture into baking pan (10 x 12) or casserole dish. Cut butter into slices and distribute it evenly throughout the mixture (put the butter slices into the juice).

The piecrust has a decorative border around the edge. With a knife remove the border. Cut piecrust in 1" strips and lay across the top of cobbler mixture in a lattice design. If you don't know what that looks like, then just lay it crisscross over the top, and it will bake just fine. Bake for 50 to 60 minutes or until golden brown.

Remove and let cool a little. Serve warm with vanilla ice cream. Yum-yum!

Advanced

Pour mixed ingredients in casserole dish. Distribute butter slices evenly in mixture. Cut piecrust in 1" strips and lay in lattice design.

Bake. Remove from oven and let cool. Serve with vanilla ice cream.

2

What's the Point?

~

hy should you cook? What compelling reason could be given that would motivate you on a daily basis? Those questions have countless answers, but let me begin by saying that it will bless your heart and revolutionize your household! God meets us in the kitchen when we go there looking for Him. It is a time of spiritual renewal as we utilize our kitchen time to fellowship with the Lord. A divine appointment awaits us daily, and if you keep that appointment, you will find that the kitchen will become a place you run to for more of God.

Finding God in the kitchen alters our thinking and renews our motivation to meet Him there. Why would God wait for us in that room? When we approach it with the proper attitude He knows:

- we're looking forward to spending time with Him. James 4:8 says, "Come near to God and he will come near to you."

- we desire for Him to minister to us in a special way. "Call to me and I will answer you and tell you great and unsearchable things" (Jeremiah 33:3).

  We also long to have a servant's heart. "Whoever wants to become great among you must be your servant" (Matthew 20:26).

How many of us would be in the kitchen cooking if it weren't for others? A salad, sandwich or diet drink would probably do us just fine. But when we submerge ourselves into a plan for a delicious meal to be presented in an attractive way, we are esteeming others higher than ourselves, and that excites God. The attitude and commitment to serve invites Him to be with us.

> *God* meets us in the kitchen when we go there looking for Him.

Women who know how to cook but don't like cooking have missed the significance of their time in the kitchen. Serving delicious food may satisfy the appetites of the recipients; however, both the cook and those fed will be robbed of the extra special blessing that comes when the preparer understands the purpose of cooking.

Think for a moment of meeting with a girlfriend for fellowship. You could gather in the lobby of a hotel or a beautiful park so you could have a good conversation but where do you usually meet? That's right, in a restaurant. Why? Because there is something special that takes place over food. And when the meal is exceptional, that makes the experience even more memorable.

Food ministers to three senses: seeing, tasting and smelling. When warm fellowship is added to the table it touches our souls. Edifying conversation ministers to our hearts, and pleasant music makes the dining experience grow even richer. A wonderful lunch with a close friend leaves us feeling whole and encouraged. What if that happened consistently in your home with your family? Imagine how that would elevate your relationships to a higher level of intimacy.

Kitchen Worship

I so enjoy talking to my dear friend Michelle McKinney Hammond. The next time you are in a Christian bookstore, ask the clerk to bring up a list of the books she has written. There are so many to choose from that you can just close your eyes and point to one. No matter which one you choose, it will be a profound blessing in your life.

Michelle is single, but she understands the *why* of cooking and has given me some of my best recipes. She delights in entertaining her friends and loved ones with delicious meals. When she visits my home, I insist she teach me something new before she leaves. It was Michelle who exclaimed one day with her beautiful smile and effervescent personality, "Cooking is an act of worship!"

When Michelle made that statement she piqued my interest, and I pondered its message. The dictionary defines worship this way: "to regard with great, even extravagant respect, honor or devotion." King David was a worshiper. In Psalm 34:1 he wrote, "I will extol the LORD at all times; his praise will always be on my lips."

The kitchen is a very appropriate place to worship the Lord and to offer up prayers to an attentive God. In the quiet space of our hearts, we can both meditate on the Word of God and draw closer to the throne of grace while our hands are busy preparing a meal. Kitchen worship turns our thoughts upward to the divine Savior. No wonder so many mothers of old would go into the kitchen and sing hymns and spiritual songs as they moved around. They utilized their time by directing their attention to the Lord. Oh, let us become their students!

The kitchen is a perfect place to give thanks, offer gratitude for our family and pray for their health and strength. We can praise God daily for the food we get and the appliances we have to help us prepare it. We can rejoice over running water and the role it plays in our cooking. What about the communication and laughter that will take place around the dining room table? Each encounter brings us closer to one another as the events of the day are shared and an interesting topic of conversation is introduced and discussed. There is so much to be grateful for as we prepare a meal. The reasons to praise are endless, and God will stick around to hear them.

Many mothers complain about the lack of time for devotion in their busy day, and, indeed, there should be a period set aside for quiet time with the Lord. (I suggest you read *A Place of Quiet Rest* by Nancy DeMoss.) But here are usually almost two hours daily (preparation, serving and clean up) set aside in the kitchen that can be utilized to meet and have deep abiding fellowship with the Lord. When I enter my kitchen I look forward to experiencing the presence of God. As a result, I have untold stories of my intimate rendezvous with my living Savior. Praying for my husband and children one by one is daily fare. There are so many things to talk to God about—so much so that the food I'm preparing seems to reach completion much too soon.

> Cooking is an act of worship!

We eat in our family room on a cloth-covered folding table with beautiful place mats. I like that location because it overlooks the backyard, and the CD player in that room affords us soft, soothing music. It took a while to woo my family away from the TV and get adjusted to listening to music while eating, but now they automatically turn off the TV when a meal is about to be served. Fresh flowers often decorate the center of our table and our family time together is a sweet-smelling fragrance of fun and fellowship.

Frank and I have six children, and I wish this scenario would have been played out with all of them. Unfortunately, four of my children were grown before I learned the value of the kitchen and the importance of sharing our meals. It is, however, always a great delight when they visit and join us for meals. There is a healing and bonding power even now as we break bread together. God is faithful even in fixing our messed-up yesterdays. He is always happy to fulfill His Word to us: "I will make up to you the wasted years" (see Joel 2:25).

Let's take a break and enjoy some more recipes. Remember Danielle? One day she mentioned a meal she had prepared for her husband that included string beans. When I asked if the green beans were fresh, she replied that they were out of a can. My ten-year-old quipped, "String beans come in a can?" It was then that I realized she had never had canned vegetables. I taught Danielle how to prepare fresh string beans, to which she responded, "Is that all? That's easy."

I also taught Angelique how to prepare Garlic Chicken, and it has become a big hit with her family and friends. I think I'll throw in whipped yams, and we'll make it a dinner.

FRESH STRING BEANS

2 pounds (lbs.) fresh string beans
1 smoked turkey leg or wing
½ medium (med.) onion
Lawry's Seasoned Salt
4 small red potatoes (optional)

Preparation time: 15 min.
Cooking time: 2 hours 40 min.
Serves: 6 people

Beginners

Ask someone in the produce department if string beans are in season. Remember that produce workers will not only answer your questions, but they will teach you how to select the best fruit and vegetables. In some markets, they will also cut a piece of a fruit to taste before you buy. The string beans should be full not flat and not have brown edges.

Tear the ends off the string bean and break into three pieces about an inch long. Children five years and older can be given this job to do.

The string beans cook in water that has been flavored by smoked turkey. This means you will need to boil the smoked turkey. If you are not sure how much water that will take, put the beans in a pot, pour enough water into the pot to come to the top of the beans and pour that water into a big pot. Now put in twice as much water and add the smoked turkey. Bring to a boil and reduce to a medium flame, cover with a lid and let boil until it is back to the first level (about 1 to 2 hours). No matter how many beans you're cooking, you will only need enough water to come to the top of the beans. If you boil out too much water, you can add Swanson's Chicken Broth which comes in a can. (I keep some on hand.)

Pour smoked turkey broth over the fresh string beans and bring to a boil over a medium-high flame. Season generously over the top with Lawry's Seasoned Salt and stir. Cut the ½ onion in half and add both pieces to the string beans. Boil for 20 minutes and stir. Taste the string beans and add more salt if necessary.

If you're going to add potatoes now is the time to do it. Cut the red potatoes in half and sprinkle salt and pepper on the open side of the potato. Lay the potatoes on top of the beans and cover. The steam from the beans will cook the potatoes.

Cook beans until your desired texture (some like them firm and others soft). I usually cook mine an extra 20 minutes.

Advanced

Boil the smoked turkey part until you have enough broth to reach to the top of the picked beans. Halve the ½ onion and add to the pot. Season with Lawry's Seasoned Salt. Cook on medium heat for 40 minutes or until desired texture. If desired, add potatoes 20 minutes into the cooking.

Now how about some garlic chicken and whipped yams to go with the string beans?

GARLIC CHICKEN | RECIPE

4 boneless chicken breasts (with or
    without the skin)
salt
basil
lemon pepper
chopped garlic
extra virgin olive oil

Preheat oven: Broil
Preparation time: 10 min.
Broiler time: 15 to 20 min.

Beginners

Turn your oven on to broil (preheat). If you have a gas oven, you are going to place the prepared chicken on the bottom part of your oven underneath the flame. If you have an electric oven only the top coils will light. Put the oven rack in the middle section. The top level will broil it too fast and the bottom one too slow.

Run the chicken under water and pat dry with a paper towel. Place the chicken on a cutting board and season with salt, lemon pepper and basil (these are found in the seasoning section of the store). Sprinkle them evenly across the chicken. Once you've tasted the completed chicken you'll know how much more or less to add the next time.

Now you're going to tenderize the chicken by beating it. This will also flatten the chicken so that it cooks faster. In a kitchen supply store, you can purchase a meat tenderizer that looks like a hammer. These work very well. If you don't have one, you can use the bottom edge of a round jelly jar. (Make sure to wash the bottom first.)

Start at the edge of the chicken and start pounding. The goal is to evenly flatten the chicken breast.

Place the breasts on a cookie sheet.

Pour 1 tablespoon of olive oil in the middle of each chicken piece and spread.

Add 1 teaspoon of chopped garlic in the middle of each piece and spread evenly over the top. Fresh chopped garlic can be purchased in a jar in the produce section of the store.

Put the cookie sheet under the broiler and set the timer for 15 minutes. Check the chicken. It should be a deep, golden brown. Depending on the thickness it may take an additional 5 minutes. If you're not sure it is done, remove the pan and cut into the thickest part of the chicken. It should be white not pink. (Some stores sell special toothpicks that you can stick into the chicken to see whether it is done.)

Advanced

Season, beat the chicken flat, season, and spread 1 tbsp. olive oil and one tsp. crushed garlic over each piece. Broil until done (approximately 15 to 20 minutes). Serve immediately.

 **WHIPPED YAMS**

> 3 medium-sized yams
> butter
> Sugar in the Raw (or your preference of
>   sugar)
> optional: cinnamon, nutmeg, vanilla
>
> Preheat oven: 350 degrees
> Preparation time: 5 minutes
> Baking time: 60 min.

Beginners

Yams are different than sweet potatoes; they are darker in color. The insides should be a deep orange. You can break off a small piece of the tip of the yam to check the color. Yams grow in soil, so the outside may be a little dirty. Put each yam under running water and wash with your hands or a vegetable brush. Wrap in aluminum foil and twist the edges so the juice will not leak. Place on a cookie sheet about 2 to 3 inches apart. Bake until the yam is soft (approximately 1 to 2 hours depending on size). Test doneness by squeezing the yam. If it's soft, the yam is done.

After they've been cooked and taken out of the foil, peel the skin back by running a fork along the skin. Place yam in a bowl with 2 tbsp. of butter. Mash with a fork. Add sugar and more butter until you like the taste. Yams are naturally sweet so you may not need sugar at all. Add a little cinnamon, nutmeg and vanilla if you like those flavors, but make sure to add just a little at a time until it meets with your satisfaction.

Advanced

Bake the yams. Scoop out insides and place in a bowl. Mash with a fork and add remainder of ingredients to taste.

Good Eatin'

Good food served with a good attitude makes for good eatin' (as they would say in the South). Your family will look forward to this daily experience. By the time you have spent an hour or more in the kitchen praying for your family and meditating on the Word, you will want to feast on the Lord's answered prayer by watching what happens around the dinner table.

The ultimate purpose for preparing food is the communion that will take place while breaking bread together. Webster's dictionary says that communion is "an act or instance of sharing." The word "commune" means "to talk over or communicate intimately."

Good food stimulates quality communion and that brings about new understanding and insights into the lives of your family. A wife and/or mother who has steeped herself in prayer while preparing a meal will grow a discerning spirit as she watches the mealtime unfold. When the food is good and served in a relaxed setting, it stimulates conversation (even though you may have to be the one who gets it going). If you have a family that is not talkative, Christian bookstores have aids that encourage family discussions. You might even try putting a different, light-hearted and fun question under each dinner plate.

A person's demeanor is exposed over food. If they are upset, the tendency is to push the food around on the plate or to overeat. Or maybe a talkative member of the family is hardly saying a word while the quiet one won't sit still. A watchful wife and mother will notice changes in her family's behavior and use her prayer time to intercede on behalf of various individuals and ask for God's wisdom. Regular meals reveal whether there is a pattern taking place with that person or if, perhaps, they are just out of sorts for the day.

> *A* kitchen prayer is a mighty moving force when done regularly and in humility.

> *The* ultimate purpose for preparing food is the communion that will take place while breaking bread together.

A kitchen prayer is a mighty moving force when done regularly and in humility. The kitchen will become a sanctuary where miracles are born in the servant's heart and witnessed around the dining room table.

The kitchen is also an excellent place to pray for other people. One of the focal points in my kitchen is my refrigerator. It is covered from top to bottom with pictures of loved ones and friends. A variety of colorful and fun magnets hold this wonderful collage together. Just glancing at the refrigerator is a reminder of all the wonderful persons

I know and how important it is for me to remember them in prayer. There is so much to be accomplished in my kitchen that the only thing I regret is how little time there is to accomplish it all.

An Example

If you have children, it is wonderful to involve them in the process of preparing food, assisting in the setting of the table or cleanup while worshiping God. During the school year it may be difficult to get a lot of assistance, but summer vacation is a great time for boys and girls to join in.

If you have a CD player, music goes a long way in setting the mood. Make sure it's something the Lord would like to hear as well. Allow your children to set the table using whatever they would like to choose from in the house or garden. Start your time with a short prayer and say a word about the significance of preparing food with the right attitude. Hopefully they will have observed your cheerful demeanor while working in the kitchen and want to experience some of the joy you have found in that place. Share the vision of worshiping God in the kitchen and enjoy the fellowship with your child/children.

A very easy recipe to teach them is how to make bran muffins. Gabrielle loves these and wanted them made for her class on her eleventh birthday. Because the recipe is made with buttermilk, the batter can be stored safely for up to two weeks in the refrigerator. It's fun to bake a whole batch or just a couple at a time.

BRAN MUFFINS ━━━━━━━━━━ RECIPE

2 c. All Bran Cereal
4 c. Quaker Granola Cereal (yellow box)
5 c. flour
3 c. Sugar in the Raw (or white sugar)

2 tsp. salt
4 ½ tsp. baking soda (*not* baking powder)
1 qt. buttermilk
4 eggs
1 c. vegetable oil
2 c. water
pecan pieces (optional)
Craisins (optional)
soft cream cheese (optional)
cupcake paper shells

Preheat oven: 400 degrees
Preparation time: 15 min.
Baking time: 20-25 min.

Beginners

In a large bowl mix all the ingredients together with an electric mixer until blended well. Pour into a container and refrigerate for an hour. Put paper cupcake shells into cupcake pan. Fill cupcake shells ⅔ full (the muffins will rise as they bake).

Our family likes pecans and Craisins in the muffins. Put a heaping tablespoon of batter into the shell, add four broken pieces of pecans and Craisins and cover with another tablespoon of batter. Bake in the middle rack for 20 to 25 minutes. Muffins are best eaten when warm. Soft cream cheese is a great addition.

The fellowship with your children around the preparation, serving and cleanup can be fun. Gabrielle and I have sung songs, told jokes and splashed each other with dishwater. It's a great time to share in conversation and discuss current events. Don't be surprised if your kids open up and share parts of their heart. Some of your favorite memories just might come from your time with them in the kitchen.

3

God's Embassy

~

Our kitchen is a central room in *God's embassy*. Second Corinthians 5:20 says, "We are therefore Christ's ambassadors...." Where does an ambassador live? An ambassador lives in an embassy. In an embassy, the furnishings, art, food and music are reflections of what is taking place in the ambassador's homeland. When someone comes to "our" embassy, they should be able to feel, taste and catch a glimpse of what is going on in our homeland—heaven.

In heaven, love and peace abound. There is no confusion, bitterness, anger, hatred, jealousy or envy. Heaven is filled with the glory of God. There is also safety and refuge in our eternal home. Perhaps your earthly embassy does not reflect heaven the way you would like it to right now but you want it to. The goal of this book is to help you gather the tools necessary to accomplish that feat while, at the same time, developing a love *and* appreciation for cooking.

Understanding that our dwelling place is God's embassy is humbling because emulating heaven on earth may seem overwhelming. However, if we want our home to become a true reflection of heaven, all we need to do is ask God for the wisdom and knowledge necessary to make it happen.

Proverbs 24:3-4 states, "By wisdom a house is built, and through understanding it is established; through knowledge its rooms are filled with rare and beautiful treasures." Our embassy should be a bright beacon light on our block whether we live in a house, an apartment or a tent. When we grasp the importance of our embassy, it will revolutionalize our priorities.

I exercise almost daily by walking up and down my block. It accomplishes two purposes: I get my much needed exercise and it allows me to speak to my neighbors. One day as I was walking up the block, one of my neighbors pulled alongside me. I noticed she was in a different car so I asked, "Where is your car?"

"My car was stolen out of my front yard the other day. I loved that old car!" she sadly exclaimed. Then she continued, "When I realized it was gone the only thing I could think of was to come to your house. I rang the doorbell but you weren't home."

> *Our* kitchen is a central room in *God's embassy*.

This wonderful lady is of a different faith but we have become friends. As she drove off I rejoiced in knowing that she sees my dwelling as a refuge where she can come when life gets hard. Whenever I make a pound cake, some of the first slices go to this dear neighbor. She also loves my Curry Chicken. (These two recipes are in the back of this book.) I hope when people visit our home that they leave feeling encouraged emotionally, mentally and physically.

I often hear wives say that they don't know what God is calling them to do in life. That answer is found in 2 Corinthians 5:17-18,20:

> Therefore, if anyone is in Christ, he is a new creation; the old has gone, the new has come! All this is from God, who reconciled us to himself through Christ and gave us the

ministry of reconciliation....We are therefore
Christ's ambassadors, as though God were
making his appeal through us.

Our first ministry is to *reconcile* the world to God. That
begins with our husband, then children and then the world.
The word "reconcile" is defined as "harmonize," which
means "to restore to friendship."

Husbands First

Your husband may be a Christian but is Jesus his friend?
The root word of friend means "to love." Jesus made it clear
in John 14:15, "If you love me, you will obey what I
command." Do you see your husband going contrary to the
Word of God? Do his decisions consistently violate God's
principles? Then he needs to be *reconciled* to God. If Jesus
is his friend, then you can stimulate that friendship to go
even deeper.

If you had two girlfriends who were at odds with each
other and you desired to see the friendship restored, would
you take sides? Of course not. You would add a healing
balm by pointing out the good in each person and attempt-
ing to get the two of them together. Lunch would be great
but it couldn't just be any old restaurant. Ambience would
be important—a lovely décor and soft music. Great food
would also enhance the meeting.

In order for reconciliation to take place you would have
to get the two of them talking to one another. That wouldn't
happen if you dominated the conversation, so you would
have to ask God for wisdom and direction in facilitating the
initial light chatter before turning the meeting toward deal-
ing with the impasse. I've discovered that most conflicts can
be resolved with just one good conversation and a dish of
fine food. Likewise, friendship between your husband and
the Lord can be restored or strengthened. What better way

for it to take place than in God's embassy! With the right ambience and words (less is more), your husband can be inspired to turn his heart toward his friend, Jesus.

First Peter 3:1-2 states: "Wives, in the same way be submissive to your husbands so that, if any of them do not believe the word, they may be won over without words by the behavior of their wives, when they see the purity and reverence of your lives." So powerful is the influence of a wife that she can sway the quality of her husband's relationship with the Lord without speaking a word of instruction! A husband is so affected by his wife's attitude (even when he appears to be indifferent or callous) that a woman with a pure and reverent spirit can deeply impact the direction of his life. And this includes an unsaved husband.

> Our first ministry is to *reconcile* the world to God, and that begins with our husband, then children and then the world.

Our greatest challenge as wives is our tendency toward fixing our husbands instead of providing the ambience in our embassy that promotes discussion between him and Christ. So many times we are the distraction—not the proprietor—of peace. That usually comes from our desire to control any and all situations. If Jesus and our husbands were talking on the telephone, we would be the static on the line making them miss significant messages to one another. That can all change when we realize we have been called to the ministry of reconciliation.

The ministry of reconciliation is ongoing, and our kitchen ministry follows closely behind.

Kitchen Ministry

Have you ever talked to women about their various ministries? Some work in the areas of children, youth, marriage, family, hospitality and more. How many women have ever told you they have a kitchen ministry? Can you count them on one hand? How about one finger? And yet a kitchen ministry is one of the most powerful ministries in our world today. Why? Because no matter who you are or where you live, people need to eat daily!

Before we talk about this, let's make a snack. You can make it in a small portion for yourself; however, it is also fabulous for a social gathering.

CHIPS & DIP   RECIPE

tortilla strips
Philadelphia Cream Cheese (whipped)
salsa (your favorite)

Preparation time: 5 min.

Beginners

Buy an appetizer tray that has a bowl in the middle. You can find nice decorative ones made out of plastic. Philadelphia Cream Cheese comes in a solid rectangle or whipped in a tub. Purchase the *whipped* cream cheese. Put 3 heaping tablespoons in the middle of the bowl and pour salsa over it. Place a teaspoon in the mixture so your guests can spoon it out. Pour tortilla strips around the appetizer tray. I suggest you keep these ingredients on hand in case unexpected guests drop by. You will love this combination. It is so easy to make and delicious.

Advanced:

Cover cream cheese with salsa in a bowl and surround with tortilla strips.

Variation: Put tortilla strips on a plate and sprinkle shredded cheese (prepackaged with three different cheeses) over the top. Place in microwave for one minute and serve with salsa.

Our kitchen ministry not only blesses our family, it also reaches out to others. Frank, my husband, received a call from an out-of-town couple who were struggling in their marriage. It was decided that the husband would fly in and spend three days with Frank. This husband and Frank barely knew each other, and this highly educated and professional man had his apprehensions.

The ministry of reconciliation is ongoing and our kitchen ministry follows closely behind.

Frank met with him at his hotel for two days and then suggested he come over to our home for dinner the next evening. I called Mike (not his real name) and gave him a choice of entrées and desserts. I could hear appreciation in his voice as we set the menu.

Preparing the embassy required not only that it be clean (like heaven) but that it be filled with pleasant smells and sounds. When Mike arrived with Frank, I met them on the front porch. I'll never forget when Mike stepped into the living room. He stopped, looked around and released a sigh as if he had entered a refuge. I gave him several choices of drinks and he and Frank hunkered down on the sofa for a discussion while I finished the meal.

I prepared a spring garden salad with cubed mango and sweet grapes. For dinner we had grilled lamb chops, whipped yams and asparagus. Dessert was banana pudding. Mike said the lamb chops were the best he ever had and asked for the recipe.

RECIPE LAMB CHOPS

1 rack of lamb (individual chops)
salt
pepper

garlic salt
Monterey Steak seasoning (Shilling)

Preheat oven: Broil
Preparation time: 10 min.
Broiler time: 10 min.

Beginners

Lamb is expensive, but it's wonderful as an extra treat and great for a small dinner party. Lamb is best when bought fresh in a rack (that means all the chops are joined together). Ask your butcher to cut each chop individually. (That means each chop should be separated from the other.)

Preheat oven to broil. The broiler rack should be in the middle of the oven.

Lay lamb chops flat and lightly sprinkle with salt, pepper and Monterey Steak seasoning. Sprinkle garlic salt on each chop but make it heavier than the previous seasonings. Work the seasoning into the meat by gently rubbing the seasoning into each piece with your fingertips. Turn the chop over and repeat on the other side. You can adjust how much seasoning you will use after you have tried the finished product once.

Place the lamb chops on a cookie sheet and put in the broiler for 5 minutes (rare), 8 minutes (medium rare) and 10 to 12 minutes (well done). The thickness of the chops will determine how long it cooks. You can remove the cookie sheet and cut into the lamb chop to see when it is broiled to your satisfaction.

Advanced

Season lamb lightly with seasonings making the garlic salt the heaviest seasoning. Massage seasoning into lamb and broil on the center rack. An average cut lamb chop will be well done in 10 to 12 minutes.

Mike also said that the banana pudding tasted just like an aunt's dessert he had loved while growing up. He recounted that his aunt was a horrible cook but she was famous for one thing—banana pudding. Our dessert brought back fond memories for him.

While Frank and Mike were driving back to the hotel, Mike called his wife and told her to think about what it would take to make the marriage work. I believe the combination of Frank's counsel over those three days coupled with the hospitality created an environment that helped Mike look at his life and marriage from a different perspective.

Would you like to sample that wonderful banana pudding?

 **BANANA PUDDING**

2 c. milk

2 pkgs. vanilla pudding mix (Jell-O)

1 can condensed milk (Eagle Brand—green can)

1 small Cool Whip (reduced fat)

1 box Nilla Wafers (Nabisco low fat)

1 cream cheese (⅓ less fat—rectangle size)

4 ripe bananas (sliced ¼")

Preparation time: 15 minutes (chill in refrigerator 1 hour before serving)

Beginners

This is a dessert that keeps well in the refrigerator. You can make it a couple of days before your dinner, and it will still taste wonderful.

Lay out the cream cheese an hour before preparing the recipe so it can soften at room temperature.

In an 8" square pan, put one layer of Nilla Wafers along the bottom. We will also put them along the sides, but that will be done after we pour the mixture in so the wafers will stand up by themselves.

Pour 1 cup of milk into a blender, 1 package of vanilla pudding, ½ can condensed milk, ½ of cream cheese and ½ of Cool Whip. Turn blender on blend and use a spoon to gently move the ingredients around so they are all mixed together.

Pour mixture over vanilla wafers in pan.

Peel bananas and cut them into round slices. Lay them side by side (flat) on top of the mixture. Repeat the ingredients in the blender and blend. Pour this mixture over the bananas until it reaches the top of the pan. Stick wafers along the side of the pan (standing up and touching). Crumble wafers across the top for a decorator flair. Cover with Saran Wrap and chill for at least an hour before eating.

Advanced

Layer the bottom of the pan with wafers. Blend 1 c. milk and 1 pkg. of pudding with half of all the other ingredients. Pour over wafers and lay sliced bananas on mixture. Repeat recipe in the blender, pour over bananas, line sides with wafers and crumble wafers across the top.

The Kitchen Calling

A kitchen ministry is a daily calling. Your family will delight in knowing something delicious is being prepared for them, and it means even more when it's done with the right attitude and spirit. The joy and warmth that this adds to your home is immeasurable. It will take, however, a clear commitment to be consistent. But that won't be difficult because God designed women to be *relentless*. You can do it!

Why do I say relentless? Frank was riding with a CIA agent once who was a friend of a friend of ours. During the conversation, the man mentioned to my husband that in the CIA training manual, it teaches an agent what to do if they are facing a life-threatening situation with two enemy agents where one is a woman and the other a man. The manual instructs the agent to kill the woman first. Frank was shocked until the agent explained the reason behind the instruction. When Frank inquired as to the reason, the agent responded, "Because the woman is relentless."

Being relentless can be an asset or a liability, based on where it is directed. If the teachings in this book are clear, and you become relentless in your kitchen ministry, then miracles and blessings will abound. There will be a sweet peace and joy that permeates your home—but it requires you to be relentless. There will be times when you won't feel like spending time in preparation, serving and cleaning up the dishes after your family. (This is not to suggest that your children shouldn't participate if they are old enough to offer assistance.)

Proverbs 21:19 says, "Better to live in a desert than with a quarrelsome and ill-tempered wife." The Greek word for quarrelsome is "pedalion" which is defined "rudder."

We see the word "rudder" again in James 3:3-4: "When we put bits into the mouths of horses to make them obey us, we can turn the whole animal. Or take ships as an example. Although they are so large and are driven by strong winds, they are steered by a very small *rudder* wherever the pilot wants to go." No matter which way the captain of the ship turns the wheel, it is the rudder that determines the direction. And since it's *under* the ship, many times you wouldn't be able to detect that it's going in the wrong direction unless you check the compass or end up in the wrong port.

Can you see how frustrating it would be for your husband (the captain) to be leading the family in a certain direction only to have to deal time and time again with an unwilling rudder? God has given husbands the sphere of authority, but He has given wives the sphere of influence. How we use that influence greatly impacts the spirit and attitudes in our homes.

Proverbs 14:1 states, "The wise woman builds her house, but with her own hands the foolish one tears hers down." It takes relentlessness to build or tear down a house. We know the Bible is not talking literally about building or tearing down a house in the physical sense. The materials we use are words, attitudes and actions. If we are selfish, critical and judgmental, our house (marriage) will eventually come down. However, if we are edifying, encouraging and self-sacrificing, our home will be a heavenly embassy, a refuge and a harbor. If we are relentless in these things we will be blessed.

> *A* kitchen ministry is a daily calling.

I feel like cooking something, don't you? Let's make a salad.

STRAWBERRY SPINACH SALAD — RECIPE

1 pkg. fresh spinach
2 c. fresh sliced strawberries
¾ c. toasted almonds

Poppyseed Dessing:
2 tbsp. white wine vinegar
¼ c. granulated sugar
¼ tsp. Dry mustard
¼ tsp. salt
¼ c. Grape Seed oil
1 tsp. Poppy seeds

Beginners and Advanced

In small bowl whisk together vinegar, sugar, mustard, and salt. Whisk in oil. Stir in poppy seeds. Refrigerate.

Mix salad ingredients together and toss with dressing. This salad was so good that I had two helpings and was tempted to pass on the entrée. You will love it. Thanks, Irene.

Your family will delight in knowing something delicious is being prepared for them and it means even more when it's done with the right attitude and spirit.

4

Getting It Straight

~

*I*f God wants wives and mothers to minister to their families from the kitchen, then why is it so few of us know how or have the interest? When I speak at a women's conference, I usually ask women who know how to cook *and* love it to stand. Normally 25 percent or less rise to their feet.

God's Word on this issue is straight and direct. It is right to assume then that at some point the path got crooked. I believe the turn began in my generation. My mother had dinner on the table at 4 P.M. every day. I can still hear my father coming through the front door with a familiar whistle as the smell of dinner led him to the table. During dinner he continuously told jokes, and my siblings and I had a secret pact not to crack a smile. When we finally couldn't hold it in anymore, there was an explosion of laughter. It is one of my favorite remembrances of childhood.

When I got married I didn't carry on that tradition. Why? Because I never learned how to cook, and my husband was not a jokester. There wasn't a lot of chatter around the table; dinnertime left me feeling empty. It never dawned on me that my own family was different from the one I grew up with, and that didn't make it worse, it only made it different. There were a lot of precious memories waiting but I lacked both the wisdom and knowledge to uncover them.

When I was growing up in the 50s and 60s, women were beginning to leave their homes to find fulfillment in the workplace. Credit cards became a new road to financial debt, and many families found their bank accounts stretched to the limit. What was the answer to the problem? Two-income families. With the mother working outside the home, dinner became the exception, not the rule. The working mother was tired after an eight-hour day and had little time or interest in building a kitchen ministry.

I would like to talk more about this subject but let's do it over a hot bowl of Clam Chowder.

 ## CLAM CHOWDER

2 bottles clam juice
1 pint heavy whipping cream (in milk cartons like regular milk)
1 c. milk (2% fat)
4 cans Cream of Potato soup (Campbell)
1 can cream corn (Del Monte)
5 small cans minced clams
1 medium-large yellow onion
6 slices pork bacon
salt
white pepper

Preparation and cooking time: 1¼ hr.

Beginners
You will be so pleased with how easy this recipe is to fix. It was taught to me by the husband of a dear friend of mine.

Chop onion in ¼" pieces

Cut the bacon in half so it fits easily into the skillet. Brown the bacon on a simmer. You want the bacon to be brown but limp.

Remove the bacon and add onion to the bacon grease and simmer. Cover the skillet with a lid and stir the onions occasionally. The onions are white when they are first cut but become clear in the skillet when they are done. The flame should still be on simmer. The cooking term for this is *sauté*. While the onions are simmering, cut the bacon into pieces the size of the chopped onions.

Open the cans of minced clams and drain the juice out of the can. Add clams and bacon to sautéd onions, cover for 4 minutes.

In a large pot add the clam juice, milk, heavy whipping cream, cream of potato soup and cream corn. Stir well. Add the onions, clams and bacon mixture and stir well. Bring to a boil and drop the flame to a simmer. Add salt and white pepper a little at a time until it satisfies your taste buds.

Important: Stir the soup every 5 minutes for 45 minutes or until it reaches desired consistency. Use a big spoon that will allow you to scrape the bottom of the pot while stirring. A Teflon-coated pot is ideal. The milk will burn at the bottom if you do not stir deeply.

Delicious!

Advanced

Brown bacon on a simmer. Remove and chop. Sauté chopped onions in bacon grease. Add drained minced clams and simmer 4 minutes.

Add remainder of ingredients to a large pot and stir well. Add bacon, onion and clam mixture. Bring to a boil, simmer 45 minutes or until desired consistency. Stir often, scraping bottom of pot to prevent scorching.

There is something about a hot bowl of soup, especially on a chilly day. Perhaps you're allergic to clams but can eat seafood. I suggest you cut up some fresh pieces of your favorite crab or fish (boneless) and simmer in the chowder mixture for approximately 20 minutes or until done.

48 • God Is in the Kitchen Too

This recipe is greatly complemented by hot, buttered French bread or sourdough bread.

RECIPE — HOT BREAD

1 long thin loaf French or sourdough bread
1 stick butter (room temperature)

Preheat oven: 400 degrees.

Beginners

Use a sharp knife to cut bread slices. Don't cut all the way through, just deep enough to spread butter in between the slices.

Spread some butter on each slice, and place loaf in the middle of a piece of aluminum foil. Fold the foil up along the sides but don't seal if you like your bread crunchy.

Place bread on cookie sheet and put in oven for 5 minutes.

Advanced

Slice bread and spread with butter. Bake 5 minutes.

Now Is the Time

We can't change the past. It would have been wonderful if we had been taught the joy and purpose of cooking as we were growing up, but most of us did not have that experience. Now is the time for us to come into that understanding, take our rightful place and change our destiny!

Preparing meals in the kitchen is an investment of time that will require you to subtract energies out of other areas where you are currently directing your focus. It is important to note, however, that this investment pays very high dividends. Watching the positive, ongoing development of your family unit is priceless. Your family will grow to cherish the times around the dinner table and develop an inner stability they would not have without it.

"But, Bunny," you might say, "I enjoy working outside my home. Can't I do both?"

Good question. The answer is yes—once you have carefully considered the following list and have been able to check off each one:

List of Priorities

___*Time with the Lord*

How does your day start? Are you in perpetual motion from the time you wake up until the time you go to bed? If so, you are too busy. Whether your quiet time with the Lord is in the morning or evening, it is a necessary time that allows us to focus and commune with our living Savior. Are you spending time alone with God daily?

___*Embassy is clean, organized and maintained*

Our home, God's embassy, should be clean, organized and maintained. Do you think heaven is clean? Can you imagine God dispatching an angel on your behalf and the angel tripping over a box on the way to get to you? Our embassy is a reflection of heaven, and cleanliness and organization should be a priority. It takes *time* to properly maintain a home; it is a daily task. Perhaps you can afford to pay someone to take care of this job. Usually only a small percent of women have that luxury. The rest of us need to accept cleaning and organizing as our responsibilities.

Caring for your home also includes the beautification of our yards. Heaven should begin the moment someone steps onto our property. Is the lawn manicured? Has thought been given to the landscaping? Does the porch and front door welcome family and visitors? Taking care of the yard takes *time*. (I hire a gardener to cut the grass.) Perhaps you live in an apartment and don't have to concern yourself with yard responsibilities. That will free up some of your time.

Remember that the upkeep of your yard and home directly affects the property value of your neighbor's house. It is a good witness to increase our neighbor's equity because we take the time to care for our residence.

___Daily quality time with our husbands

It is important that we connect with our mates daily. So many times husbands and wives are like two ships passing in the night. Providing an atmosphere to talk takes *time* and *desire*. Preparing a delicious dinner goes a long way in setting the stage for discussion. Connecting doesn't have to take a long time, but it is a necessary part of each day.

No two days are alike. What was different about your spouse's day today? You say he doesn't want to talk? Then check your style of communication. Are you wordy, critical, judgmental and a complainer? Or is your "speech seasoned with salt" (Colossians 4:6)? Do you make him thirsty to hang around and listen to your words of reverence, encouragement and edification? One of a man's greatest desires is to be known, appreciated and loved by another person. That is why he married you, so make it a priority and give it some time. It may happen only in one minute intervals, but it will eventually happen if you ask God for wisdom in communicating with your spouse.

___Physical intimacy is a priority

In my book *God Is in the Bedroom Too,* I write about the importance of satisfying, physical intimacy between a husband and wife. When a wife thinks up her schedule for the day, this seldom makes the list. That is not to suggest that this should happen on a daily basis (for some it does), but it does suggest that it is a consideration. It is difficult to enjoy physical intimacy when you are exhausted. So many wonderful things come out of that time together, and it should be a priority. That means putting the children to bed early enough to free up some of your evening time.

___*Daily quality time for children*

How much quality time do you think each of your children needs a day? I'm speaking of uninterrupted time where you are focused only on that child and his or her concerns, hopes and dreams. I give Gabrielle, my ten year old, at least 30 minutes a day. If I had more children at home I would probably drop it to 15 minutes per child, but quality time would not be an option in my schedule.

When Gabrielle comes down the stairs in the morning, I am waiting at the bottom with a warm housecoat (just taken out of the dryer). She smiles as she slips into its warmth. I wrap her up in my arms and lead her to the living room sofa. The lighting is soft, and soothing music is softly playing. I pray for her day and then begin telling her how special she is by naming as many of her good qualities that come into my mind. Most of the Scriptures Gabri has learned have come from our time together in the morning as I quote them over her.

One morning I asked Frank to wake Gabrielle and get her moving toward preparing for school. It was late when I came downstairs, but the first thing she did was go to the sofa and wait for me there. She wasn't going to miss our time together!

When I pick Gabrielle up from school, our conversation in the car is quality time. Before she asks me to put on her favorite gospel CD, I ask the question, "On a scale of 1 to 10, how was your day today?" Almost every day is a 9 (a point being taken off because she thinks the weather was either too hot or too cold). We talk about what she did in each class, and I ask a variety of questions. If she is having a problem or challenge, I want to know about it and that takes *time*.

Putting Gabri to bed closes off our quality time. After she prays, Gabri gets into bed and lays flat on her back. She counts to three and we begin to wrestle. My objective is to give her a kiss on her lips, and her goal is to make sure that doesn't happen. We roll and tumble and laugh and often end up in a pillow fight. She wakes up in the morning and goes to bed with a smile on her face and that takes *time*. Spending daily quality time with our children cannot be assigned. We have to be there.

___*Children's activities are a priority*

If you have preschoolers it goes without saying that they demand attention. You can put them into daycare while you go to work but always remember that whatever is learned by them there, positive and negative, will be a part of who they are for the rest of their lives. The teachers or instructors will move on, but you'll continue to deal with the residual impact.

The five years prior to kindergarten are precious and can never be regained. The children's first smiles, steps and words are precious memories to be opened time and time again. I believe mothers should hold the opportunity to experience those things dear to their hearts and do what it takes not to be robbed of those moments.

Once the children are in school we're still not off the hook. For stay-at-home moms, schools need volunteer support in classrooms, the PTA and other areas. There are also open houses, back to school nights, athletic competitions, plays and so much more that requires our *time* and *attention*.

___*Emergency preparation*

This is the scenario: You and your husband go out for dinner. A storm rolls in and the electricity in your house goes out. Do your children know where you keep the flashlights?

What if your child plugs something into an electric socket and it shorts out causing a fire. Are there fire extinguishers handy and have your kids been taught how to use them?

Do you have fire drills (and earthquake drills if you live in that type of area)? Do you have a meeting place outside your home if you get separated?

Do you have medical release forms completed on your children so that thorough instructions can be given to those who care for them on a temporary basis? Do you have extra water and emergency supplies stored away? Are your important papers together in one place? Have you established a second trust designating who would take care of your children in the event of a simultaneous death of you and your husband?

Emergencies happen and, by definition, they come unannounced. As the ambassador of your embassy it is imperative that you address these issues and that takes *time.*

Time spent on church and its activities, with extended family members, friends and neighbors are also part of the list. Can you see how difficult it is for a wife/mother to work outside the home? If it is your desire to stop working and come home, then ask God for wisdom and He will give it generously (see James 1:5-6). Titus 2:4 says that it's God's desire that we be "busy at home...." Be patient and let God work out the details.

Now, I'm ready for some hot chicken soup. Are you?

CHICKEN VEGETABLE SOUP

6 fresh chicken drumsticks
3 lg. boxes Swanson's regular chicken broth
½ russet potato
2 carrots
1 can kernel corn (drained)
⅛ head cabbage
½ onion

vegetables and herbs of your choice
granulated chicken boullion or salt

Optional
pepper
rosemary
basil
thyme

Preparation time: 2 hours

Beginners

This soup makes the whole house smell good, and it's especially nice on a cold or rainy day. I suggested the vegetables my family prefers, so feel free to add or subtract the ones you like or dislike most.

Pour chicken broth into a large pot.

Wash chicken legs (yes, you can use white meat but I use the legs because the meat is more tender when it is cut away from the bone and put back into the soup). Put the chicken into the chicken broth.

Cut ½ onion in half and add both parts to the broth. Boil chicken on a medium-high flame for an hour. Remove chicken and let cool.

Some vegetables take longer to cook than others so add the carrots and potatoes first. Slice the carrots approximately ½" wide. Cut the potatoes in ½" cubes.

Boil carrots and potatoes for 10 minutes. Add sliced cabbage, corn and other vegetables of your choice. Boil for 20 minutes.

Remove skin and bones from chicken legs and cut chicken in bite-sized pieces and add to soup.

The Swanson's Chicken Broth is already salty, so taste the soup to determine whether you want to add additional salt. Rather than adding salt, I prefer to add granulated chicken bouillon. Pepper, basil, rosemary or thyme are some additional seasonings you may want to add. Open the jar and smell the seasoning—that will help you decide whether you would like to add it to your soup.

Advanced

Boil chicken in Swanson's Chicken Broth until done. Remove and let cool. Add desired vegetables and cook. Skin and debone chicken and return to the pot. Add desired seasonings.

Variation: Instead of using all vegetables, add your favorite pasta.

Time

After considering the list of priorities you may feel frustrated. Perhaps you've worked very hard to reach your position in your job. Maybe you have achieved a degree from higher education and want to use it, or you are an entrepreneur and have people working for you. Coming home to minister to your family may appear quite complicated and cause you to feel anxiety. Aren't you glad that God has everything under control?

First, Philippians 4:6-7 says: "Do not be anxious about anything, but in everything, by prayer and petition, with Thanksgiving, present your requests to God. And the peace of God, which transcends all understanding, will guard your hearts and your minds in Christ Jesus." All you have to do is want to work it out, and it will be up to God to provide the way.

But what about all the hard work and effort you've put in at the workplace? You may have struggled hard to reach your position. That reminds me of Romans 8:28: "And we know in all things God works for the good of those who love him, who have been called according to his purpose." Don't be surprised if God shows you how to do some of that work out of your home. If you are a professional person with clients, then you can determine how many you will see and when. If you provide the "want to," God will provide the "how to."

Also, get ready to be laughed at and ridiculed by those who don't understand the redistributing of your time. Unless a person has an eternal vantage point they most likely will not be able to comprehend your decision to be at home. Remember, as children of the living God we are eternal time travelers. Psalm 90:4 says one day with the Lord is like a thousand years on earth. If we were to break down that equation, it would mean that by the time we live to be 75 years old only 1 hour and 48 minutes have passed in heaven. We can't keep living as if earth is our only home. The decisions we make here will determine the quality of our time in heaven. It's 2003 and I am 53 years old, which means I probably have about 20 minutes of heaven's time left to complete the work God has called me to do. It's so easy to understand why Moses said, "Teach us to number our days" (Psalm 90:12).

When I counsel women who want to quit their jobs, I always remind them that they must do so with the blessing of their husbands. God has given him the right to make the final decisions concerning their home. (If that just made the hair stand up on the back of your neck, then read my book *Liberated Through Submission*. Scripture teaches that submission is a positive, powerful and aggressive principle designed by God for every man and woman, single and married. A simplistic definition is "submission means God intervenes.") Most women I have counseled who wanted to come home against their husbands' desires have been off their jobs within a year. And it's God's glory because it was not done in human power or might but by God's spirit.

Now, since we've fixed soup, how about adding a Caesar Salad to go with it?

CAESAR SALAD

1 bag of Romaine lettuce salad mix
1 bag croutons
5 anchovies
⅓ c. olive oil
1 coddled egg
1 tbsp. Parmesan cheese
1 tbsp. minced garlic
1 tsp. mustard
2 tbsp. Worcestershire Sauce
1 tbsp. juiced lemon
salt (dash)
pepper (dash)

Beginners and Advanced

Put desired number of croutons in bottom of bowl. Pour Romaine lettuce over the croutons to soften.

Combine the rest of the ingredients in a blender, add to lettuce and toss.

Note to beginners: Anchovies come layered in a can. Lift out one piece at a time and use 5 single pieces.

Note: How do you make a coddled egg? Put an egg, still in the shell, in a cup of water and heat in the microwave for 1 minute.

My family members are not beef eaters; however, if you enjoy beef, this is a great recipe from my mother. This will complement your soup and salad.

7-BONE ROAST

7-bone roast
1 pkg. Lipton Onion Soup Mix
1 can Campbell's *Golden* Mushroom soup

Heavy duty aluminum foil
Preheat oven: 300 degrees
Cooking time: 3 to 4 hours

Beginners

Call your supermarket to ask whether they carry a 7- bone roast. If so, have them put one aside for you. (A 3 lb. roast will feed 4 people.)

Remove the roast from the package and run under water to wash it. Tear 2 pieces of foil 2 feet long and lay flat, criss-crossing each other. Place the roast in the center. Sprinkle onion soup mix across the meat. Pour undiluted Golden Mushroom soup over the meat as well.

Join the two ends of one strip of foil over the top of the meat and fold down in one inch creases until it reaches the top of the meat. Do the same thing with the other piece of foil. Make sure there are no openings.

The meat will cook in its own juices. Put in a casserole dish and bake a minimum of 3 hours (4 hours for well done).

Advanced

Put onion soup mix and Golden Mushroom soup across top of meat. Seal tightly with foil and bake a minimum of 3 hours.

 **BAKED POTATOES**

russet potatoes
butter
sour cream
scallions (green onions) chopped (use
green stem only)

Preheat: 300 degrees
Cooking time: 1 to 2 hours (depending on
    size)

Beginners and Advanced

Scrub the potatoes with a vegetable brush under running water. Wrap individual potatoes in foil and place on oven rack next to the roast. Test doneness by squeezing the sides of the potatoes. Should be soft to the touch. Cut down the middle and add butter, sour cream, scallions and other condiments as desired.

Feeling Good

Have you ever noticed how people gravitate toward the kitchen? The pleasure of smelling and tasting something delicious, along with encouraging fellowship, ministers to the whole person. Has a good meal ever picked up your day? When the prophet Elisha was running from Jezebel and lay exhausted by a river, God sent ravens to feed him (see 1 Kings 17:6). When Jesus called out to the disciples in the boat, He was cooking fish on the river bank (see John 21:3-12). (That could have been the second reason Peter jumped into the water and swam ashore!) When the two men on the road to Emmaus recognized Jesus after He had risen from the dead, it was *after* they broke bread together (see Luke 24:13-32).

Why did God give us taste buds anyway? He could have just given us the desire to eat in order to strengthen our bodies. Why the sweet, sour, bitter and spicy sensations? Do you think I know the answer to that question? Well, I don't. I just know that God is good and His ways are past finding out (see Romans 11:33). I figure, however, if He went out of His way to create pleasant eating sensations, shouldn't I go out of my way to see that those sensations are satisfied? I think so. What about you?

A kitchen ministry is an awesome calling and the rewards are great. The opportunities for creativity are endless. Perhaps this is what my friend Michelle meant when she said, "Cooking is worship." Once you see the smiles and satisfaction on the faces of those you feed, there will only be one thing left—to glorify God.

5

Potiphar's Mistake

~

For a long time I thought cooking was boring, and that was a mistake. I wrote this book so women could learn from my poor judgment. I'd like to share with you the following lesson.

As I was growing up, I wanted to learn from my own mistakes. You see, I was different from anyone else—or so I thought. When I became a young adult and was warned not to get into debt, I ignored the recommendation. The credit card companies started asking for my business, and they proved too tempting to resist. Once the bills were made, I struggled each month to pay them. I cared nothing about a good credit rating. You probably already know what happened. When I decided to buy a car, my poor credit rating made it difficult to acquire one, and when I did I had to pay a higher interest rate.

The Bible teaches we should "put away childish things" and realize there is a lot to learn from other people's mistakes. Potiphar is one such person who taught me a valuable lesson. The wisdom garnered from this story has had a profound impact on my life.

In the book of Genesis we find a man named Jacob who has 12 sons. The eleventh son, Joseph, was the first child born to his second wife, Rachel, whom he loved dearly. Jacob favored Joseph (one of the cruelest things we can do to our children), so his older brothers resented him.

In Genesis 37, Joseph's brothers conspire to kill him, but, instead, they decide to sell him to some traders passing by. In chapter 39 beginning in verse 1, Joseph is purchased by Potiphar, an Egyptian. Let's follow along with this story:

> Now Joseph had been taken down to Egypt. Potiphar, an Egyptian who was one of Pharaoh's officials, the captain of the guard, bought him from the Ishmaelites who had taken him there. The LORD was with Joseph and he prospered, and he lived in the house of his Egyptian master.

Even though Joseph was now a slave, Scripture says the Lord was with him and gave him success in everything he did. Potiphar put him in charge of his household, and entrusted to Joseph's care everything he owned.

> From the time he put him in charge of his household, the LORD blessed the household of the Egyptian because of Joseph. The blessing of the LORD was on everything Potiphar had, both in the house and in the field. So he left in Joseph's care everything he had; with Joseph in charge, he did not concern himself with anything except the food he ate.

So what could go wrong? We never learn the name of Potiphar's wife, but she just couldn't leave Joseph alone! Starting in verse 6 it says:

> Now Joseph was well-built and handsome, and after a while his master's wife took notice of Joseph and said, "Come to bed with me!" But he refused.... And though she spoke to Joseph day after day, he refused to go to bed with her or even be with her (verses 6-8,10).

Now you would think Potiphar's wife would just be happy with her new-found prosperity. She could valet park when she went to the mall, and there was no limit on her credit cards. But noooooo, she had to have Joseph. She was very cunning and the story reveals how she worked her plan.

> One day he went into the house to attend to his duties, and none of the household servants was inside. She caught him by his cloak and said, "Come to bed with me!" But he left his cloak in her hand and ran out of the house (verses 11-12).

Potiphar's wife is humiliated, and, as the saying goes, there is no fury like that of a woman scorned. If she had considered the cost of her actions and how it would affect her household in the future, she probably would have reacted differently. But she was embarrassed, hurt and rejected. Verse 13 says:

> When she saw that he had left his cloak in her hand and had run out of the house, she called her household servants. "Look," she said to them, "this Hebrew has been brought to us to make sport of us! He came in here to sleep with me, but I screamed. When he heard me scream for help, he left his cloak beside me and ran out of the house."

You can imagine how upset Potiphar was when he returned. His wife kept Joseph's cloak beside her until her husband came home. Then she told him this story:

> That Hebrew slave you brought us came to me to make sport of me. But as soon as I screamed for help, he left his cloak beside me and ran out of the house (verse 17).

When Potiphar heard the story his wife told him, saying, "This is how your slave treated me," he burned with anger. So Joseph's master took him and put him in prison. Joseph never returned to Potiphar's house.

This story fascinated me. There was something very strange going on. I wasn't surprised that Potiphar's wife lusted after Joseph. The Egyptians worshiped idol gods and immorality was rampant. What made this story so unusual was Potiphar's profession: "Potiphar, an Egyptian who was one of Pharaoh's officials, *the captain of the guard"* (verse 1).

Potiphar was the king's bodyguard. No, he was more than that. He was the *captain* of the bodyguard. That means he was the best of the best, and he probably was the overseer of the other bodyguards' training. Why does this make the details of this story so strange?

Have you ever seen bodyguards protecting the president of a country? When they're standing in a crowd of people, are the bodyguards looking at the president? No. They keep their eyes fixed on the crowd. What are they on the look-out for? Quick body gestures that could represent an attack and faces of criminals they've memorized. Perhaps possible assailants have dyed their hair or cut off their mustaches. Most of all they watch people's eyes because they are the window to the soul.

Now that we're adults it's time to "put away childish things" and realize there is a lot to learn from other people's mistakes.

A bodyguard is also trained in knowing every rumor, piece of gossip or complaint. They are constantly updated with the state of affairs. It is up to them to determine what is or is not threatening to the president. So this presents a question. How is it possible that Potiphar, who was the most highly trained of all the body-guards in the pharaoh's court, didn't know that his wife was lusting after another man day by day in his own house?

I guess you could say he "dropped his guard" when he came home each day. What Potiphar so excellently gave to the king, he neglected to bring home, and so he lost his blessing. I doubt his wife ever told him the truth, so he would have died never knowing how he was robbed of God's gift to his household.

My Turn

Potiphar's story is acted out over and over again in the lives of countless people. For many years I was making Potiphar's mistake. Gifts, talents and energies I so willingly shared with the world just didn't seem to make it home to my family. If my boss asked me for a cup of coffee, I would eagerly jump up and get him one. If my husband requested a glass of water, I was irritated and begrudgingly retrieved it.

I remember how fastidious I was with my work area on the job. It was important that my desk was clean at all times and only the paper I was working on at the time would be present. I needed to be able to put my hands on what was wanted immediately. Not so with my house. I owned five pairs of scissors because I couldn't find one when I was looking for it.

My patience was long at work and short at home. Common courtesies extended to coworkers or friends seemed to come effortlessly but was such a strain with my family. I prided myself on anticipating the needs of my employer, while my husband's needs went unmet. I had the same type of willing exuberance at church. I was making Potiphar's mistake, and I could have lost my blessing. That doesn't mean my marriage had to come to an end, but it could have become fruitless and meaningless.

What are your strengths? Do you handle other people's finances excellently yet the state of your personal affairs is in shambles? Or maybe you work in a ministry at church that requires you to serve other people selflessly, and once you get home that same love and kindness evaporates. Think about what you give of yourself to the world, and then inquire as to whether you also bring those gifts home to your family. Are your husband and children resentful about the amount of time and energy you give to other people and causes? If so, it's not too late to learn from Potiphar's mistake.

And then there is the issue of making mistakes with ourselves. Do you give great thought about what you're going to wear to work, church or for outside engagements? And yet at home maybe you wear the same old thing over and over again. Perhaps you think combing your hair is an option and give very little time to your appearance at the house. That's a big mistake.

Gifts, talents and energies I so willingly shared with the world just didn't seem to make it home to my family.

What about the generous compliments you pay to other women concerning their physical attributes and qualities? You admire so many of their physical traits, yet when you look in the mirror the image staring back has so many faults. If only your hair were thicker or longer, your eyes, nose and mouth larger or smaller. And then there is the issue of your body parts! Oh, if you had been God, things about you would look quite different! Once again this is making Potiphar's mistake. The admiration we so freely give to others, we neglect to bring home to ourselves.

I'd like to encourage you to bring all your compliments and adorations home to yourself. In Psalm 139:13 it says, "For you created my inmost being; you knit me together in my mother's womb. I praise you because I am fearfully and wonderfully made."

Were God's knitting needles broken when He made you? Did He purchase the material necessary to complete the task from a secondhand store? Perhaps He was having a really bad day when He decided on the features of your face or the shape of your body! Or maybe—just maybe—you were made perfect for His plan.

I think the last statement accurately identifies God's purpose for your life. You were "fearfully and wonderfully made." There is something good about every feature you have if you'll stop letting the world be your measuring stick. When you delight in your own individual beauty, a transformation will take place. We need to place an appreciation in us for our existing qualities. Make sure you bring your attention and encouragement home to yourself and you will be blessed. (This is not to suggest that we can't accentuate or heighten our natural resources.)

Once we acknowledge that we need to bring our gifts home and the kitchen ministry is a calling, the next step is obedience. It can mean the difference between living or dying. Whether it's a dream, goal or relationship, obedience to God's principles makes the difference. I learned from Potiphar's mistake. What about you?

Let's Cook

Whew! That brief Bible study made me hungry. Let's make some grilled salmon, mashed potatoes and asparagus. This meal looks so pretty arranged on the plate. When it's complete, a mound of mashed potatoes will go in the middle, the strip of salmon lays across the potatoes and four pieces of asparagus are draped over the salmon in criss-cross fashion. I do hope you can see a picture of that in your mind.

 **SALMON**

1½ lbs. fresh salmon
butter
salt
pepper
garlic salt

Preheat oven: 400 degrees
Preparation time: 10 min.
Cooking time: 25 min.
Feeds: 4 to 6 people

Beginners

Purchase your salmon in the fresh seafood department. Ask the clerk to cut off the skin and cut the fish in 2" strips.

Wash the fish and pat dry.

Season with salt, pepper and garlic salt. (Make the garlic salt the heaviest seasoning.) Rub the seasoning into the fish gently with your fingertips.

Lay each individual piece on a sheet of heavy-duty aluminum foil. Place two generous pats of butter on top and fold the foil securely down from the top and on the sides. Fold it in such a way that it will be easy to unfold. Place the "salmon pockets" on a cookie sheet.

Bake for 20 minutes.

Salmon comes in different depths so after 20 minutes you will need to check to see if it is done. Open the foil (be careful not to burn yourself with the steam) and look at the fish. It should have changed from red to pink.

Remove the fish from the oven and fold back the foil in such a way as to create its own personal holder (or bowl). There will be liquid in the bottom created by the fish and the butter. Spoon the liquid over the fish (this is called basting).

Turn the oven up to broil and place the rack on the top setting. Put the fish under the broiler for one minute, and then remove and baste. Put back under the broiler for another minute or two. The salmon should now be a golden brown.

Advanced

Cut salmon in 2" strips. Season with salt, pepper and garlic salt (be more generous with the garlic salt). Massage into fish. Place two pats of butter on fish. Seal each piece in heavy-duty aluminum foil and bake 20 minutes.

Open foil to create the fish's own container. Baste salmon and put under broiler for one minute. Baste again and brown under broiler.

ASPARAGUS

asparagus
salt

Preparation time: 5 min.
Cooking time: 10 min.

Beginner and Advanced

Asparagus comes with a green crown on top and a long stalk. Cut off 1" from the bottom part of the stalk. In a pan wide enough to hold the asparagus, add 1" of water, 1 tsp. of salt and bring to a boil. Add asparagus and cover with a lid. Cook until desired texture. (I like mine just a little tender.)

 **MASHED POTATOES**

3 russet potatoes
1 stick butter
salt
pepper
milk

Preparation time: 10 min.
Cooking time: 45 min.

Beginners

Scrub skin of potatoes clean.

Put in pot, cover with water, add 1 tsp. salt, boil until potatoes are soft (the skin of the potatoes will split open).

Drain water off potatoes.

Use a fork to scrap skin off potatoes.

Put one stick of butter in a bowl and put hot potatoes on top of the butter. Sprinkle in salt and pepper. Use electric mixer to mash the potatoes. If you desire creamy potatoes, add milk a little at a time until it reaches your desired consistency.

Advanced

Skin boiled potatoes. Mix with butter and seasonings.

Add milk for creamier texture.

Your dinner guests will think they've just eaten at a five-star restaurant! Just in case you have some chocolate lovers in your group, the following recipe is very simple but will please your chocolate-loving friends.

DERBY PIE

1 c. sugar
6 tbsp. flour
1 c. semi-sweet chocolate chips
1 ½ tsp. vanilla
2 eggs
½ c. melted butter
1 c. pecan pieces
1 Pillsbury Pet-Ritz Pie Crust

Preheat oven: 325 degrees
Preparation time: 10 min.
Baking time: 50 to 60 min.

Beginner

Mix dry ingredients together. Add eggs, melted butter and vanilla. Pour mixture into pie crust. Tear off a 1" strip of aluminum foil and cover the border edge of the pie. (This keeps the edges from burning.) Bake for 50 to 60 minutes.

Serve warm with vanilla ice cream (Häagen Dazs).

Advanced

Mix ingredients and pour into pie shell. Bake for 50 to 60 minutes.

6

Ready, Set, Go!

~

*W*hoa! I know you're chomping at the bit to start your *kitchen ministry,* but before you leave the gate you're going to need a plan. Without it you'll get halfway down the track and faint because of the daily demand of this task. To run this race effectively you need organization in your meal planning and in your kitchen.

How many times do you go to the grocery store in a week? Calculate how long it takes to drive to and from the store and the amount of time it takes you to do your shopping. Add it up and if it totals more than an hour, it means there is extra time you're about to add to your free-time column. Do you ever find yourself walking up and down the aisles trying to figure out what you're going to have for dinner? Does that make you feel anxious, angry, agitated, frustrated and more? Well, you can kiss those emotions goodbye!

The following is a fool-proof plan that will eliminate meal planning confusion forever. At the beginning of each week you will reach for your meal chart that has a list of everything you know how to cook. This chart is broken down by specific meats, fish, vegetables, starches, desserts and miscellaneous items. I love giving this list to my husband to make the meal selection for the week. First he looks at the meat or fish section and makes his choice, then next comes the vegetables and starches. We go day by day. He gets what he wants, and I don't have to rack my brain with meal planning. Sometimes when he's too busy to participate, I use the list, and it makes organizing the meals for the week a breeze. You can also allow your children to make some of the selections. As an example, the following is my list (you'll notice pork and beef are missing—that is my family's dietary choice):

Meats

Chicken

__ Baked chicken
__ Garlic chicken
__ Fried chicken
__ Smothered chicken
__ Curry Chicken
__ Chicken salad
__ Chinese chicken wings
__ Chicken and dumplings
__ BBQ chicken

Soup

__ Chicken
__ Clam chowder
__ Navy bean

Vegetables

__ Asparagus
__ Cabbage
__ Greens
__ Fried corn
__ Corn on the cob
__ Broccoli
__ String beans
__ Steamed vegetable medley
__ Spinach

Meats cont.

Lamb

__ Lamb chops

Fish

__ Baked fish w/mango
     sauce
__ Fried fish
__ Baked salmon

Salad

__ Caesar
__ Spring garden
__ Potato
__ Salad w/balsamic
     vinaigrette
__ Spinach
__ Salad w/roasted
     chicken
__ Tuna

Starch
__ Macaroni & Cheese
__ Rice
__ Baked potatoes
__ Country-fried potatoes
__ French fries
__ Whipped yams
__ Candied yams
__ Red russet potatoes
__ Mashed potatoes

Miscellaneous
__ Bran muffins
__ Spaghetti
__ Cornbread
__ Homemade rolls

Dessert
__ Peach cobbler
__ Carrot cake
__ Pound cake
__ German chocolate cake
__ Banana pudding
__ Derby pie

The following is a sample menu list for my family representing one week:

Monday
Spring garden salad
Garlic chicken
String beans
Rice

Tuesday
Pecan crusted sand dabs w/mango sauce
Mashed potatoes
Greens
Salad w/balsamic vinaigrette

Wednesday
Baked chicken & dressing
Cabbage
Fried corn
Homemade rolls

Thursday
Salad
Lamb chops
Whipped yams
Broccoli/asparagus

Friday
Fried fish
Corn on the cob
Spinach
White beans
Corn bread

Saturday
Leftovers

Sunday
Baked turkey and dressing
Greens
Candied yams
Macaroni & cheese

Once my menu for the week is complete, I go into the kitchen and make up my grocery list by determining what ingredients are necessary for each meal. I check to see what I already have in stock and only pick up from the store what is needed. The only reason to return to the store later is for the meat and fish that will be prepared at the end of the week. Setting up this process will take a little time, but the effort will be well worth it. You'll ultimately save many hours.

So, let's get started. Fill out the following list with the meals you know how to cook. Don't be disappointed if you're looking at an almost blank page; I regularly add to my list by

I know you're chomping at the bit to start your *kitchen ministry,* but before you leave the gate you're going to need a plan.

learning new recipes. Write down what you'd like to learn how to cook and begin today by contacting a friend who knows how to prepare it. Set an appointment to meet with him or her to show you how to make the dish. Use the blank recipe pages at the back of this book for your convenience. Remember to follow your friend around the kitchen and write down everything he or she does. Prepare the recipe in your kitchen as soon as possible. You can also try some of the recipes in this book:

Chicken   **Beef**

Fish   **Pork**

Lamb   **Vegetables**

Starch   **Miscellaneous**

Dessert

Once you get in the habit of making up your menu for the week from your list, you'll never want to return to the everyday guessing game. Also, watch your family's delight when you write out your weekly menu and post it on the refrigerator. They will look forward to dinnertime.

Kitchen Organization

Now let's take a look at your kitchen. Since you're going to be spending a great deal of time in this room over the course of your life, wouldn't it be wonderful to operate in a place free of clutter and confusion? That will be difficult to accomplish if your kitchen is disorganized. Remember when I shared with you about the concept of God's embassy? Your kitchen is one of the rooms in His embassy, and it needs to be clean and organized. If you just let out a groan, it means that the idea of that task is overwhelming and unpleasant. It's my job to make this process painless. We're going to rearrange your kitchen one day at a time. You will need to buy 3 boxes with lids and handles on the side, the kind you purchase at a moving store or packing outlet, along with 3 index cards (I got this method out of Emilie Barnes' book *More Hours in My Day*). Follow these easy steps.

First

Assess your kitchen. Open every drawer and cabinet one at a time. Is it organized or cluttered? Do you have utensils, pots, dishes or seasonings you hardly ever use? Do you find yourself constantly hunting for a particular item when you're cooking? That is about to change.

Second

The goal is to do only one drawer or cabinet a day. If a couple of days pass in between times that is all right as well. Keep a trash bag, box and index card handy. Number the first box and index card #1. Everything you put into the box is to be written on the card so you will be able to retrieve it when necessary. Once you close the box and put it away, you only have to look at the card to find its contents (put the cards in a secure place). Items you don't need can be put in one bag to give away, and trash goes into the other bag. If you do a little every day the task becomes a cinch.

In my kitchen I have 9 cabinets and 8 drawers, which means in 17 days I can have a completely clean and organized kitchen—and it only takes minutes a day! The key is to put up items you don't use very often and throw away or give away what you don't need. If you have to move cooking utensils around in a drawer to find what you want when you're cooking, it means the drawer is too cluttered.

A kitchen store will have organizers for your supplies. Where do you keep your foil, Saran wrap and storage bags? You can get an organizer that attaches to the inside of one of your cabinet doors that stands them straight up and thus frees up additional space in a drawer or cabinet. There are all kinds of fun organizers.

Third

Organizing your seasoning is a special project all itself. You will save a considerable amount of time when you can immediately put your hand on any seasoning you need. I have a seasoning carousel that sits on my counter and spins revealing the different seasonings. There are also seasoning racks that can be attached to a wall that display the most common seasonings. My additional seasonings are alphabetized in a cabinet (this takes a little time but once it's done you never have to do it again).

Approaching the Kitchen

Almost every day you will have the pleasure of approaching the kitchen. Gone is the dreading and foreboding attitudes because you know God is in there! Let's learn another recipe, and then I'll tell you more of what is waiting for you in that special room. My daughter in college requests this recipe be waiting for her when she returns home from school (along with a peach cobbler).

RECIPE — CHINESE CHICKEN WINGS

2 pkgs. chicken wings

BBQ sauce
1 bottle Bulls Eye BBQ sauce
¼ c. light brown sugar
½ capful white vinegar
1 tsp. granulated chicken bullion
1 dash Worcestershire sauce
1 pinch dry mustard
1 dash Tabasco sauce
Lawry's Seasoned Salt
pepper

Preheat oven: 500 degrees
Preparation and cooking time: 1 hr. 45 min.

Beginners
Wash the chicken and tuck tip under drumette piece (see Chapter 1, Fried Chicken recipe for instructions on this technique). Season chicken lightly with Lawry's Seasoned Salt and pepper. Place on cookie sheet and bake until golden brown (approximately 25 to 30 minutes).

While chicken is baking, pour BBQ sauce ingredients into a saucepan. Stir well and bring to a simmer. It is important to add ingredients according to your taste. You might want it spicier, so add more Tabasco sauce; you might like it sweeter, so add more brown sugar. If you want it saltier, add more chicken bullion.

Remove chicken from oven and reduce heat to 325 degrees. Put chicken into a Pyrex dish or pan. Pour BBQ sauce over the chicken and cover with lid or aluminum foil.

Bake for 30 minutes, remove from oven and spoon sauce from bottom of pan over chicken. Replace cover and return chicken to oven for an additional 30 minutes.

Advanced

Season chicken lightly with Lawry's Seasoned Salt and pepper. Bake chicken at 500 degrees for 30 minutes. Combine sauce ingredients in a pan. Put chicken into a Pyrex dish, pour on sauce, cover and bake at 325 degrees for 1 hour. Baste after 30 minutes.

Finger lickin' good!

Let's add a vegetable with this chicken. I find that many people cringe when I say spinach, but this recipe is so good even your children will be clamoring for more. It uses only seasonings, but is extremely flavorful. I recommend you buy the spinach prewashed and bagged in the produce section of your store. If they do not carry this, purchase fresh spinach.

SPINACH

4 bags fresh baby spinach (prewashed)
½ medium onion
¾ stick salted butter
Accent seasoning salt

Beginners and Advanced

Slice onion thinly. Melt butter in large pan over medium heat. Add onion and stir approximately 5 minutes until tender (the goal is not to brown the onion, just to cook until tender). Add the bags of spinach and reduce flame to a simmer. Sprinkle generously with Accent. Cover pot for 10 minutes and stir. Increase flame to medium high and cook spinach, stirring often. Spinach will create it's own liquid. Cook spinach until the liquid has been reabsorbed into the spinach (approximately 30 minutes).

7

Kitchen Meditations

~

Now that the kitchen is streamlined and your meal planning is organized, let's turn our direction toward your kitchen meditations. This is going to revolutionize your life! Even though you may have morning devotions, setting time aside to meditate on God's Word cultivates faith, hope and power.

David reflects on the benefits of meditation in Psalm 1:2-3. It says:

> But his *delight* is in the *law of the LORD,* and on his law he meditates day and night. He is like a *tree* planted by *streams of water,* which yields its *fruit in season* and whose leaf does not wither. *Whatever he does prospers.*

Do you believe the Scripture you have just read? Then, based on your belief, you will be motivated to act. Following this chapter will be 52 kitchen Scripture meditations. There is one for each week of the year. Notice I call them meditations not memorizations. There is a difference. One is hidden in the heart, the other is remembered by the brain. Scripture says, "I have hidden your word in my heart that I might not sin against you."

The eating habits of a cow teaches us the principle of meditation. When a cow bites off a clump of grass it goes down into the first of its four stomachs. The grass is regurgitated and comes up. This is called the cud. The cow once again chews the grass and it goes into its second stomach. This cycle is repeated until it reaches its fourth stomach. By then the grass is liquid and easily absorbed into its system.

The Word of God is so rich and deep that it cannot be comprehended with casual reading. It requires meditation. Your daily kitchen ministry is going to afford you the time and allow you to indulge in pursuing a deeper walk with God. You will find yourself longing to experience the deep and abiding fellowship that flows from your kitchen. Thus I have designated only one Scripture per week. It takes that amount of time to glean and catch a glimpse of God's intention for that particular Scripture. I have selected Scriptures that I feel will deeply impact your relationship with God, your family and the world.

The first kitchen meditation starts on page 94. It is Psalm 1:2-3. To help you get started, I'll go through this one with you. Notice that specific words or phrases have been emphasized. To get a deeper understanding, these words need to be defined and then reflected upon. In the rest of the meditations I will not be defining the words for you because I want you to thirst for a deeper understanding of Scripture yourself. You should acquire the definitions during your daily devotion time and then use them during your kitchen meditations. The tools you will need are a dictionary and a concordance. The first highlighted word is "delight." The Scripture reads, "In His *delight*..." Webster's dictionary says delight means "to take great pleasure, to give keen enjoyment, to give joy or satisfaction to." This means that what you are about to embark upon is not drudgery but a pleasure.

What occurrences in your life have been a delight? What childhood memories make you smile? Perhaps your high school or college graduation brought you great joy. Maybe

it was your wedding or the birth of your first child. Based
on the definition of "delight," you should meditate on how
the word applies in your personal life. When we do so,
God begins to formulate illustrations and examples that
help us better understand the meaning of Scripture.

The other resource material that will be helpful in meditation is a concordance. When you look up a specific word
in a concordance, it gives you every Scripture listed in the
Bible that uses that word. In the Strong's exhaustive concordance, the word "delight" comes up more than 50 times.
Can you see why this research needs to be done during
your devotional time? As you begin to cross reference Scripture, it takes you deeper into the mind of God. (Kay
Arthur's *How to Study Your Bible* will be a great tool to aid
you in this process.)

We're about to take delight or enjoyment in a particular
thing which is the law of the Lord. The law of the Lord is
God's commandments and directives. The dictionary
defines law as "a rule of conduct or action prescribed or
formally recognized as binding or enforced by a controlling
authority." Psalm 119:92 states, "If your law had not been
my delight, I would have perished in my affliction." As I
mediated on the "law," my mind drifted to this particular
Scripture because, while writing this book, I lost the ability
to type because of a physical challenge with my right hand.
As I meditate on the one Scripture, it reminds me of others
I have hidden in my heart that bring me joy. See how it
works!

We are to find pleasure in God's laws because they are
binding and true. Once we accept that God went out of His
way to give us laws and commandments for our *benefit,* we
begin to look upon them with delight.

Psalm 1:2-3 continues by saying that we will be like a
"tree." As I meditate on that word without even opening up
the dictionary, I ponder on the fact that the Bible didn't say

I would be like a flower, a bush or grass because all of those have shallow roots. He says I will be like a tree. Webster's dictionary says a tree is "a perennial plant having a *single* elongate (long) main stem generally with few or no branches on its lower part." My, my, my! I could spend a few days in my kitchen just thinking about this definition. Palm trees have always fascinated me because I learned that the harder the wind blows the deeper its single root extends into the ground. We are connected directly to God through His Son Jesus—and that stem runs long and deep. There are other trees whose branches are wide and far reaching that provide shade from the heat and shelter from the storm. It definitely takes a day in your kitchen to meditate on the word "tree."

Notice that this "tree" is not planted in a garden or on a lawn; it is planted by "streams of water," where it can be replenished and refreshed daily. From meditating upon God's living Word, we become like that tree established by streams that flow from an ever full reservoir that regenerates itself. It never runs dry, even when your body is wracked with pain and you are inundated with troubles on end. Though the heat from the trials of everyday living are beating down upon you continuously, joy and peace is ever present, bubbling briskly and powerfully just beneath the surface. Life flourishes on its banks, and our future is the fruit of its faithfulness. Cast all doubt aside and wait for it.

"Which yields its fruit in season" signifies that we will bear fruit. You can count on it. The dictionary defines fruit as "a product of plant growth." For many years I longed to be full of wisdom, knowledge and discernment. I soon discovered that it doesn't happen just because you want it; it is the result of growth. My pastor, Dr. E.V. Hill, says you can't ripen a peach with a blowtorch. You have to allow the sun (Son) to shine on it and go through the process. When we accept that fruit is the product of our lives, it gives us the patience to endure. That patience produces hope. Romans 8:24-25 states: "But hope that is seen is no hope at all. Who hopes for what he already has? But if we hope for what we do not yet have, we wait for it patiently." Do you see how the Scriptures overlap? As you begin to commit more and more Scriptures into your heart, your kitchen mediations will grow richer and richer.

The last portion of this Scripture, "whatever he does prospers," should keep you happy the whole time you are cooking dinner. Think about it, my friend, God's Word promises us that when we meditate continuously on it prosperity follows. The word "prosper" is defined as "to succeed in an enterprise or activity: to become strong and flourishing." This Psalm 1:2-3 kitchen meditation will bring rest to your soul. No longer do you have to strain and press to achieve and accomplish goals. God will give you the wisdom and knowledge to satisfy the desires of His heart for your life.

I started you out with using only the dictionary and a concordance. There are some wonderful Bible study computer programs my husband, Frank, runs while studying the meaning of particular Hebrew words and their root origins. Once you begin meditating on God's Word, your thirst for knowledge will be unquenchable. Don't worry, we will never be able to exhaust the depths of Scripture!

We've Only Just Begun

It's almost time for you to go into your kitchen and prepare a meal. Hopefully, you already know what you are going to prepare and all of the ingredients were acquired at the beginning of the week. Even before you enter that God-designed refuge, offer up a prayer unto the Lord and ask Him for wisdom in maximizing your time while cooking. Once you are in the kitchen, open this book to your kitchen meditation and the journey begins. The Sriptures are set in large type so you can read them easily as you move around the kitchen. Don't be surprised if your friends marvel at your spiritual growth. They most assuredly are going to want to know what in-depth Bible study you've been attending.

Cooking, serving and cleaning up is a physical activity, so don't become alarmed if you get tired. Serving God is work, but I can promise you, you may "get tired in it" but never "tire of it."

Journaling your kitchen experience is also rewarding. As you look back in the years to come, you will marvel at your growth.

By now you should be ready to take on an involved recipe. Let's make some baked chicken and dressing. (For the holidays you may want to replace the chicken with a turkey.)

Corn bread dressing freezes so well that once you've learned how to make it, I suggest you double the recipe and freeze it in meal-sized freezer bags. I usually get five extra meals of dressing out of it, and all I have to do after that is bake the chicken. Don't let the length of this recipe scare you. It actually is very easy. However, if you are planning to serve this for guests, I recommend you prepare the dressing a day or two in advance.

 **CORN BREAD DRESSING**

Note: It takes four separate steps to make the dressing: 1) baking the corn bread, 2) making the broth that will be poured over the crumbled corn bread, 3) adding the chopped vegetables to the corn bread and 4) combining the first three steps.

> *Corn bread*
> 2 c. yellow cornmeal (Albers brand)
> 2 c. flour

2 tbsp. baking soda
2 tsp. salt
½ c. Sugar in the Raw (or white sugar)
2 c. milk
⅔ c. corn oil
2 eggs

Preheat oven: 400 degrees
Preparation time: 10 min.
Approximate baking time: 25 to 30 min.

Follow step 1

Broth for corn bread dressing
2 fresh turkey parts (legs or wings)
1 med. onion
3 stalks celery
½ small green pepper
½ bunch scallions
salt
pepper
sage

Follow step 2

2 bunches of celery
2 green peppers
2 onions
1 bunch of scallions

Follow step 3

Beginners and Advanced

I suggest you prepare the dressing *before* baking the chicken. Set 2 cups of uncooked dressing aside to stuff chicken. Some people recommend not stuffing the chicken because of the potential of salmonella poisoning. Frank loves the dressing in the chicken, and we haven't had that problem, but I wanted to pass on the warning.

Here are the 4 steps to making corn bread dressing:

Step 1: Corn bread

In large bowl mix all the corn bread dry ingredients well. In another bowl use a mixer to blend the milk, eggs and oil. Pour liquid into dry mixture and stir together until well blended. Pour into lightly oiled 9" x 12" Pyrex dish and bake.

Step 2: Broth

Put two fresh turkey legs or wings in a large pot and fill with water. Add one onion (quartered), and ½ green pepper. Add three stalks of celery cut in half and ½ bunch of scallions (dark green part only). Shake salt and sage generously over the top of the water. Shake half that amount of pepper in the water. Bring to a boil and cook covered over medium flame until water is boiled halfway down.

Step 3: Dressing

Chop all the vegetables, add ¼ cup of vegetable oil to skillet. Pour in vegetables and cover with salt, pepper and sage generously. Cover and simmer until onions are clear.

Step 4: Combining all ingredients

Crumble the corn bread into very fine pieces. (If you have children, they will love this assignment.) Pour sautéd vegetables into crumbled corn bread. Remove turkey and vegetables from broth. Slowly add broth to the corn bread and mix well. Dressing should be moist but not soupy. Pour dressing into greased Pyrex dish and bake at 400 degrees until golden brown.

BAKED CHICKEN

whole fryer chicken
salt
pepper
sage
Reynold's Oven Bag

Preheat oven: 325 degrees
Preparation time: 10 min.
Baking time: 3 hrs.

Beginners

Remember, the yellow color means the chicken will be fresher and more tender.

There is an open cavity at one end of the chicken. Reach in and remove the giblet pieces (liver, kidney, neck) and set to the side. Wash the chicken inside and out with running water. Pat outside of chicken dry with paper towels.

Season generously with salt, pepper and sage. Massage the ingredients into the skin of the chicken.

Optional: Stuff the chicken with dressing in the inner cavity.

Put 1 tbsp. flour in medium-size roasting bag (the flour keeps the bag from exploding once it gets hot). Place chicken inside and seal the bag with a twist tie.

Bake the chicken at 325 degrees until it's a deep golden brown. When you cut the chicken, the juices should run clear.

I don't know about you but I like gravy on my meat and dressing. This gravy is easy to make.

RECIPE   GRAVY

2 lg. boxes Swanson Chicken Broth
Wondra flour
pepper
granulated chicken bouillon
Kitchen Bouquet gravy coloring

Preparation time: 5 min.
Cooking time: 20 min.

Beginners and Advanced

Bring two boxes of chicken broth to boil on high heat. I suggest you save ¼ box of chicken broth in case you add too much flour and need to add more liquid. Stir in Wondra flour until the broth is thick like gravy. The flour will form lumps in gravy.

Pour gravy through a strainer into another pot. Add pepper to taste. Add a few drops of Kitchen Bouquet gravy coloring. If salt is needed, add granulated chicken bouillon.

Since you're in the kitchen anyway, let me suggest that you make the most of your time and throw some chicken into the gravy. Simmer it for an hour, and now you have "smothered chicken," which can be refrigerated or frozen and served as another meal over rice or mashed potatoes.

RECIPE   SMOTHERED CHICKEN

chicken pieces
salt
pepper
vegetable oil

Preparation time: 10 min.
Cooking time: 1 hr.

Beginners and Advanced

Season chicken with salt and pepper. Heat ¼ cup of vegetable oil in skillet until very hot. Braise the chicken (the goal is to brown the chicken at a very high heat without cooking it on the inside). Add to gravy, cover with lid and simmer. Stir frequently and deeply along bottom of the pot to prevent sticking

It's Been So Good

Who would have ever thought that I, Bunny Wilson, would do a cookbook? Surely not me—and definitely not my family. It just goes to prove what God can do when we walk in His Word, way and will for our lives. When I surrendered my life to Christ, I was not an author, a speaker or a teacher. I wonder where God will lead you? It's been good sharing out of the depths of my heart the joy and peace that comes from serving the Lord.

I pray that you will get the most out of the Meditations as you serve the Lord in the kitchen. Following the meditations are more recipes for you!

Write to me after you make any of the recipes in this book and let me know how they turned out! (P. Bunny Wilson, PO Box 2601, Pasadena, CA 91102.) By the way, I would love to get one of your easy recipes. I would also enjoy reading your kitchen testimony. Additionally, I have a special request. Since you're going to be in the kitchen almost daily, please remember me and my family in your prayers.

Note: Read Chapter 7 for insights and suggestions for using these Kitchen Meditations.

But his *delight* is in the *law of the* Lord, and on his law he meditates day and night. He is like a *tree* planted by *streams of water,* which yields its *fruit in season* and whose leaf does not wither. *Whatever he does prospers.*

—Psalm 1:2-3

Definitions

Delight _____

_____

Law of the Lord _____

_____

Tree _____

_____

Streams of water _____

_____

Fruit in season _____

_____

Whatever he does prospers _____

_____

Let your *conversation* be *always* full of *grace,* seasoned with *salt,* so that you may know how to *answer* everyone.

—COLOSSIANS 4:6

Definitions

Conversation _____

_____

Always _____

_____

Grace _____

_____

Salt _____

_____

Answer _____

_____

Trust in the *Lord* with all your *heart* and *lean not* on your own *understanding;* in all your ways *acknowledge* him, and he will make your *paths* straight.

—PROVERBS 3:5-6

Definitions

Trust _____

_____

Lord _____

_____

Heart _____

_____

Lean not _____

_____

Understanding _____

_____

Acknowledge _____

_____

Paths _____

_____

Therefore, if anyone is in *Christ,*
he is a new *creation;* the old has gone,
the new has come! All this from God who
reconciled us to himself through Christ
and gave us the *ministry* of
reconciliation.... We are therefore, Christ's
ambassadors, as though God
were making his appeal through us.

—2 CORINTHIANS 5:17-18,20

Definitions

Christ _____

_____

Creation _____

_____

Ministry_____

_____

Reconciliation _____

_____

Ambassadors _____

_____

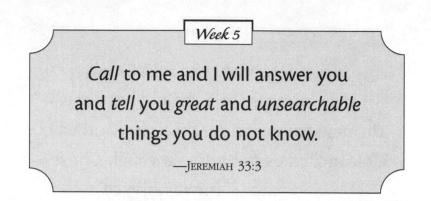

Call to me and I will answer you
and *tell* you *great* and *unsearchable*
things you do not know.

—JEREMIAH 33:3

Definitions

Call _____

_____

Tell _____

_____

Great_____

_____

Unsearchable_____

_____

Whoever *wants* to *become great* among
you must be your *servant.*

—Matthew 20:26

Definitions

Wants _____

_____

Become great _____

_____

Servant _____

_____

Note: My book *7 Secrets Women Want to Know* does an in-depth teaching on servanthood.

I will *extol* the LORD at all times;
his *praise* will *always* be on my *lips.*

—PSALM 34:1

Definitions

Extol _____

_____

Praise _____

_____

Always _____

_____

Lips _____

_____

By *wisdom* a house is built, and through *understanding* it is established; through *knowledge* its rooms are filled with rare and beautiful *treasures.*

—PROVERBS 24:3-4

Definitions

Wisdom _____

_____

Understanding

_____

Knowledge_____

_____

Treasures _____

_____

Wives, in the same way be *submissive* to your husbands so that, if any of them *do not believe* the word, they may be won over *without words* [instruction] by the behavior of their wives, when they see the *purity* and *reverence* of your lives.

—1 PETER 3:1-2

Definitions

Submissive _____

_____

Do not believe _____

_____

Without words_____

_____

Purity _____

_____

Reverence _____

_____

Note: See my book *Liberated Through Submission* for a more in-depth discussion of this topic.

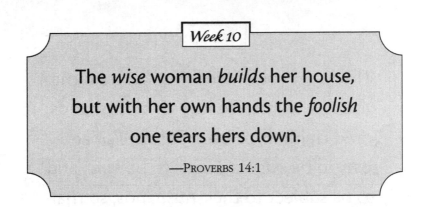

The *wise* woman *builds* her house,
but with her own hands the *foolish*
one tears hers down.

—PROVERBS 14:1

Definitions

Wise _____

_____

Builds _____

_____

Foolish _____

_____

Then they [older women] can train the younger women to love their husbands and children, to be *self-controlled* and *pure,* to be *busy at home,* to be *kind,* and to be subject to their husbands, so that no one will malign the word of God.

—Titus 2:4-5

Definitions

Self-controlled _____

_____

Pure _____

_____

Busy at home _____

_____

Kind _____

_____

And we know that in *all* things
God *works* for the *good* of those
who *love* him, who have been *called*
according to his *purpose.*

—ROMANS 8:28

Definitions

All _____

_____

Works _____

_____

Good _____

_____

Love _____

_____

Called _____

_____

Purpose _____

_____

If your *law* had not been my *delight,*
I would have *perished* in my *affliction.*

—Psalm 119:92

Definitions

If _____

_____

Law _____

_____

Delight _____

_____

Perished _____

_____

Affliction_____

_____

For *rebellion* is like the sin of *divination,*
and *arrogance* like the evil of *idolatry.*

—1 SAMUEL 15:23

Definitions

Rebellion _____

_____

Divination _____

_____

Arrogance_____

_____

Idolatry_____

_____

I *know* that you *can do all* things;
no *plan* of yours can be *thwarted.*

—JOB 42:2

Definitions

Know _____

_____

Can do all _____

_____

Plan_____

_____

Thwarted _____

_____

I [wisdom] love those who love me,
and those who *seek* me *find* me.

—PROVERBS 8:17

Definitions

I [Wisdom] _____

_____

Love _____

_____

Seek _____

_____

Find_____

_____

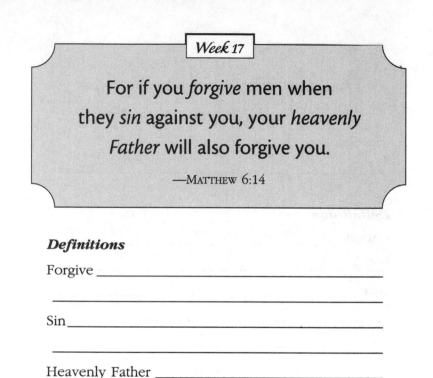

For if you *forgive* men when they *sin* against you, your *heavenly Father* will also forgive you.

—MATTHEW 6:14

Definitions

Forgive _____

_____

Sin _____

_____

Heavenly Father _____

_____

"For I *know* the *plans* I have for you,"
declares the LORD, "plans to *prosper*
you and not to harm you, plans to
give you *hope* and a *future.*"

—JEREMIAH 29:11

Definitions

Know _____

_____

Plans _____

_____

Prosper _____

_____

Hope _____

_____

Future _____

_____

If any of you *lacks wisdom,* he should *ask* God, who gives *generously* to all without finding fault, and it *will be given* to him.

—JAMES 1:5

Definitions

Lacks wisdom _____

_____

Ask _____

_____

Generously _____

_____

Will be given_____

_____

A *gentle answer* turns away wrath,
but a *harsh* word stirs up *anger.*

—PROVERBS 15:1

Definitions

Gentle answer _____

_____

Harsh _____

_____

Anger _____

_____

Behold, I am *coming soon!* My *reward* is with me, and I will give to everyone *according* to what he has done.

—REVELATION 22:12

Definitions

Coming soon _____

_____

Reward _____

_____

According _____

_____

A wife of *noble character* who can find?
She is *worth* far more than *rubies.*
Her husband has full *confidence* in her
and lacks nothing of value.

—PROVERBS 31:10-11

Definitions

Noble character_____

_____

Worth _____

_____

Rubies_____

_____

Confidence_____

_____

You are my God, and I will give you *thanks;* you are my God, and I will *exalt* you. Give thanks to the, LORD, for he is *good;* his *love endures* forever.

—PSALM 118:28-29

Definitions

Thanks _____

_____

Exalt _____

_____

Good _____

_____

Love endures_____

_____

Let love and *faithfulness* never leave you;
bind them around your neck, *write* them
on the *tablet of your heart.*

—PROVERBS 3:3

Definitions

Faithfulness _____

_____

Bind _____

_____

Write _____

_____

Tablet of your heart _____

_____

Come to me, all you who are *weary* and *burdened,* and I will give you rest. Take my *yoke* upon you and learn from me, for I am *gentle* and *humble* in heart, and you will find *rest* for your souls.

—MATTHEW 11:28-29

Definitions

Weary _____

_____

Burdened _____

_____

Yoke _____

_____

Gentle_____

_____

Humble _____

_____

Rest_____

_____

As for God, his *way* is *perfect;* the word of the LORD is *flawless.* He is a *shield* for all who *take refuge* in him. For who is God, besides the LORD? And who is the *Rock,* except our God?

—PSALM 18:30-31

Definitions

Way_____

_____

Perfect_____

_____

Flawless_____

_____

Shield_____

_____

Take refuge_____

_____

Rock_____

_____

Do not make *friends* with a hot-tempered man, do not *associate* with one easily angered, or you may *learn* his ways and get yourself *ensnared.*

—PROVERBS 22:24-25

Definitions

Friends _____

_____

Associate _____

_____

Learn_____

_____

Ensnared _____

_____

Hear, O Israel: The LORD our God,
the LORD is one.
Love the LORD your God with
all your *heart* and with all your *soul*
and with all your *strength.*

—DEUTERONOMY 6:4-5

Definitions

Heart_____

_____

Soul_____

_____

Strength _____

_____

Do you not know that your body
is a *temple* of the *Holy Spirit,* who is
in you, whom you have *received* from
God? You are not your own;
you were bought at a *price.*
Therefore honor God with your *body.*

—1 CORINTHIANS 6:19-20

Definitions

Temple _____

_____

Holy Spirit _____

_____

Received_____

_____

Price _____

_____

Body _____

_____

The LORD is my strength and my *shield;*
my heart *trusts* in him, and I am helped.
My heart *leaps for joy* and I will give
thanks to him in song.

—PSALM 28:7

Definitions

Shield _____

_____

Trusts _____

_____

Leaps for joy _____

_____

Do not wear yourself out to get *rich;* have the *wisdom* to show restraint. Cast *but a glance* at riches, and they are gone, for they will surely sprout wings and fly off to the sky like an eagle.

—PROVERBS 23:4-5

Definitions

Rich_____

_____

Wisdom _____

_____

But a glance _____

_____

Do *nothing* out of *selfish ambition* or vain conceit, but in *humility consider others better* than yourselves. Each of you should look not only to your own interests, but also to the interests of others.

—PHILIPPIANS 2:3-4

Definitions

Nothing _____

_____

Selfish ambition_____

_____

Humility _____

_____

Consider others better _____

_____

O LORD, you have *searched* me and you *know* me. You know when I sit and when I rise; you perceive my thoughts from afar. You *discern* my going out and my lying down; you are *familiar* with all my ways. Before a word is on my tongue you know it *completely*, O LORD.

—PSALM 139:1-4

Definitions

Searched_____

_____

Know _____

_____

Discern_____

_____

Familiar _____

_____

Completely_____

_____

A *fool* shows his *annoyance* at once, but a *prudent* man *overlooks* an *insult.*

—PROVERBS 12:16

Definitions

Fool _____

_____

Annoyance _____

_____

Prudent _____

_____

Overlooks _____

_____

Insult _____

_____

...the wife must *respect* her husband.

—EPHESIANS 5:33

Definitions

Respect_____

_____

I love the LORD, for he *heard* my voice;
he heard my cry for *mercy.* Because he
turned his ear to me, I will *call* on
him as long as I live.

—PSALM 116:1-2

Definitions

Heard _____

_____

Mercy _____

_____

Call _____

_____

For our *struggle* is not against *flesh and blood,* but against the rulers, against the *authorities,* against the *powers* of this dark world and against the spiritual forces of evil in the heavenly realms.

—EPHESIANS 6:12

Definitions

Struggle _____

_____

Flesh and blood _____

_____

Authorities _____

_____

Powers _____

_____

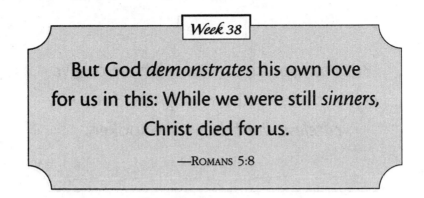

But God *demonstrates* his own love
for us in this: While we were still *sinners,*
Christ died for us.

—ROMANS 5:8

Definitions

Demonstrates_____

_____

Sinners _____

_____

But I tell you that men will have to *give account* on the *day of judgment* for every *careless word* they have spoken.

—MATTHEW 12:36

Definitions

Give account _____

_____

Day of judgment _____

_____

Careless word _____

_____

Finally brothers, whatever is *true*, whatever is noble, whatever is *right*, whatever is *pure*, whatever is lovely, whatever is *admirable*—if anything is excellent or praiseworthy—think about such things.

—PHILIPPIANS 4:8

Definitions

True _____

_____

Right _____

_____

Pure _____

_____

Admirable _____

_____

God is *spirit,* and his worshipers must *worship* in spirit and in *truth.*

—JOHN 4:24

Definitions

Spirit _____

_____

Worship _____

_____

Truth _____

_____

For as *high* as the heavens are
above the earth, so *great* is his love
for those who *fear* him.

—PSALM 103:11

Definitions

High _____

_____

Great_____

_____

Fear_____

_____

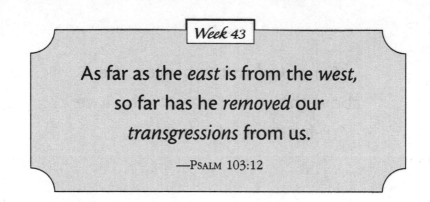

As far as the *east* is from the *west*,
so far has he *removed* our
transgressions from us.

—Psalm 103:12

Definitions

East _____

_____

West _____

_____

Removed _____

_____

Transgressions _____

_____

As a father has *compassion* on his children, so the LORD has compassion on those who *fear* him.

—PSALM 103:13

Definitions

Compassion _____

_____

Fear_____

_____

Cast all your *anxiety* on him
because he *cares* for you.

—1 PETER 5:7

Definitions

Cast _____

_____

Anxiety _____

_____

Cares _____

_____

Be self-controlled and *alert*. Your *enemy* the *devil* prowls around like a roaring lion looking for someone to *devour*. *Resist* him, standing *firm* in the faith.

—1 PETER 5:8-9

Definitions

Alert _____

_____

Enemy _____

_____

Devil _____

_____

Devour _____

_____

Resist _____

_____

Firm _____

_____

Open my *eyes* that I may *see*
wonderful things in your *law.*

—PSALM 119:18

Definitions

Open _____

_____

Eyes _____

_____

See _____

_____

Law _____

_____

Man does not *live* on bread alone,
but on every *word* that comes
from the *mouth of God.*

—MATTHEW 4:4

Definitions

Live _____

_____

Word _____

_____

Mouth of God _____

_____

He who has the Son has *life;*
he who does not have the Son of God
does not have life. I write these things
to you who *believe* in the name of the
Son of God so that you may *know*
that you have *eternal* life.

—1 JOHN 5:12-13

Definitions

Life _____

_____

Believe _____

_____

Know _____

_____

Eternal _____

_____

Offer *hospitality* to *one another* without *grumbling.*

—1 PETER 4:9

Definitions

Hospitality _____

_____

One another _____

_____

Grumbling _____

_____

The Son of Man did not come to be served, but to *serve,* and to *give* his life as a *ransom* for many.

—MATTHEW 20:28

Definitions

Serve_____

_____

Give _____

_____

Ransom_____

_____

Therefore put on the *full armor of God,*
so that when the *day of evil* comes,
may be able to *stand your ground,*
and after you have done everything,
to stand. Stand firm then....

—EPHESIANS 6:13-14

Definitions

Full armor of God _____

_____

Day of evil_____

_____

Stand your ground _____

_____

8

More Delicious Recipes

~

AMBROSIA FRUIT SALAD

2 lg. cans light fruit cocktail (Del Monte)
1 small Red Delicious apple
1 small bag of pecan pieces
½ bag small marshmallows (Kraft)
¾ small bag grated coconut
1 container sour cream

Beginners and Advanced:
   Drain the fruit cocktail, and pour fruit into a bowl. Cut the apple into bite-sized cubes. Add the remaining ingredients and mix well. Cover and refrigerate 1 hour.

BANANA SPLIT NO-BAKE CAKE

Filling
1 stick butter
2 8-ounce packages cream cheese
4 c. confectioner's sugar
1 tsp. vanilla extract
4 to 6 lg. bananas
4 to 6 c. fresh sliced strawberries
20- to 24-oz. can pineapple (tidbits or
   crushed)
whipped cream or Cool Whip

maraschino cherries
chopped nuts

Crust
2 ½ c. graham cracker crumbs
½ to ¾ stick butter (melted)

Beginners and Advanced
Crust
In a medium-sized bowl, combine crumbs and melted butter thoroughly. Spread evenly and press into the bottom of a 9 x 13-inch pan. Refrigerate the crust while preparing the filling.

Filling
Allow the cream cheese and butter to soften to room temperature. In a medium-sized bowl, mix them together with the sugar and vanilla. Using your mixer's highest speed, blend the mixture until it is smooth and fluffy. Spread it over the graham cracker crust.

Fruit Layers
Arrange the sliced bananas (thin to medium in thickness) over the entire cream cheese mixture. Completely cover this banana layer with the "mostly" drained pineapple (*Hint:* Do not fully drain the pineapple. A residual amount of pineapple juice will help keep the bananas from turning brown so quickly.) Spread the sliced strawberries over the layer of pineapple. Cover the cake with plastic wrap and refrigerate it for 4 hours or overnight.

Presentation
Cover the entire cake or each individual slice with whipped cream or Cool Whip, decorate it with the cherries, and/or sprinkle it with chopped nuts.

Serve and enjoy!

Variations & substitutions

Crust—vanilla wafer crumbs, Oreo cookie crumbs, margarine instead of butter.

Filling—reduce butter to ½ stick or omit, substitute margarine, light cream cheese; instead of vanilla use almond extract or lemon extract.

Presentation—top with toasted chopped nuts or specialty nuts (such as slivered almonds, pecans or macadamias) or with plain or toasted coconut; drizzle the whipped cream with chocolate, butterscotch or caramel syrup.

BROCCOLI CASSEROLE

1 lg. onion
1 lg. green pepper (chopped)
2 celery stalks
1 can sliced mushrooms
broccoli (fresh or frozen)
1 can Cream of Mushroom soup
1 pkg. Monterey Jack cheese

Preheat oven: 350 degrees
Preparation time: 20 minutes
Baking time: 45 min. to 1 hour

Beginners and Advanced:

Bring the broccoli to a boil in salt water, and then remove from heat. Drain it and place it in a casserole dish. Chop the onion, green pepper and celery, and sauté them in a small amount of oil. Add the sliced mushrooms, then sauté 2 more minutes. Put the soup into the pot with a little water, add the cheese and melt it. Pour this mixture over broccoli.

Bake until tender.

RECIPE CHINESE CHICKEN SALAD

This recipe was shared at one of my mentoring fellowships by one of the ladies in attendance. I like the way she broke it into sections:

> 1 to 2 lbs. boneless chicken breasts
> 1 to 2 bags Romaine lettuce and Iceberg
>   lettuce
> 6 green onions
> sesame seeds
> dry mustard
> sesame seed oil
> seasoned salad rice vinegar
> fried wonton strips
> white sugar
> almonds

> Preheat oven: 400 degrees
> Cooking time: 1 hour

Beginners
First the chicken

Bake the chicken breasts in a pan with a lid for 40 minutes. When the chicken cools, shred it. (While the chicken is cooling, make the fried wonton strips.)

Then the Salad

Place both bags of lettuce mix in a large bowl. Cut up the green onions into small pieces—only the dark green part should be used. Mix the green onions and lettuce together. Add the shredded chicken to the bowl, and mix it all together well. Sprinkle sesame seeds and almonds over the entire salad.

Dressing

In a smaller bowl mix together the sugar, dry mustard, sesame seed oil and rice vinegar. Mix and taste. (To make more dressing, repeat the same recipe over and over until you have enough. Don't try to double the ingredients to save time—instead, repeat the process each time.)

Fried Wontons

Slice a package of uncooked wonton wraps into strips. Cover the bottom of a large skillet with oil. Heat the oil until it is really hot. Then reduce the heat under the skillet and begin to cook the wonton strips in the hot oil. As soon as the wonton strips turn brown take them out and drain them on paper towels. Mix them into the salad.

Enjoy!

CURRIED CHICKEN

Michelle McKinney Hammond taught me this recipe. We had so much fun in the kitchen together!

1 pkg. chicken wings
1 pkg. chicken legs
curry powder (Sharwood's mild)
curry powder (Sharwood's hot)
1 lg. sliced onion
Wondra flour
Lawry's Seasoned Salt
black pepper
sugar
cooking oil

Sauce
Swanson's Chicken Broth
curry powder (mild)
curry powder (hot)
crushed dried red peppers

chicken bouillon
bay leaf
Worcestershire sauce

Beginners

You'll notice there are some measurements missing on the ingredients listed above. That's because Michelle doesn't measure when she cooks! So I'll do the best I can to walk you through this. Just experiment and have a good time with it.

Rinse off the chicken under running water, pat it dry, and lay it out on wax paper. Generously season it with Lawry's Seasoned Salt and black pepper. (The reason you can afford to be so generous on the seasoning is because you're also going to rub the seasoning very well into each piece of meat, and a lot of it comes off on your hands [wear rubber gloves].)

Place the chicken in a large pot with the sliced onions on top. Cover the chicken well with the mild curry powder and then use half that amount of the hot curry powder (curry stains your hands so keep those gloves on). Use two large, long metal spoons to mix the curry power and onions together. Let this mixture sit for an hour. Then sprinkle in more mild and hot curry powder and mix it all up again with the spoons.

I use two cast iron skillets for this next step. If you don't have them, use what you have available.

Cover the bottom of both skillets with cooking oil and heat it to very hot. Sprinkle in a handful of sugar. With tongs, remove the chicken and sear it (when you sear meat, the goal is to brown it quickly on the outside but not cook it on the inside). When the chicken is brown on both sides, remove it from the skillet and return it to the pot. Do not fry the onions.

Gravy

In another pot, add 3 large boxes of Swanson's Chicken Broth. Bring to a boil. Add ½ teaspoon of crushed red peppers, a bay leaf, a dash of Worcestershire sauce and chicken bouillon to taste. (Bouillon is salty so you stop seasoning with it when you like the taste. The same goes for the crushed dried red peppers. Remember, this chicken is eaten over rice and the rice will absorb some of the seasoning.)

Once the broth starts to boil, start pouring in the Wondra flour. I turn the container upside down and continue to pour until the broth thickens like gravy (I usually hold out a cup of broth so I can dilute it if I put in too much flour). Stir constantly with a large metal spoon. Remember the gravy will thicken as the chicken cooks in it, so lean more to the thin side.

Once the desired texture is reached, add the chicken and onions and let it simmer on medium-low heat for 1 hour. Stir often (every 10 to 15 min.) and scrape the bottom of the pot. (The flour settles on the bottom and will burn if not stirred properly.) Try to stir the chicken with the intention of each piece staying on the bone. Cook until the chicken is done and serve with Coconut Rice.

COCONUT RICE

1 can coconut milk
2 ½ c. jasmine rice
1 tablespoon salt
1 can plus 1 c. water

In a Pyrex dish combine the rice, water, coconut milk and salt. Mix it well and microwave it on high for 23 minutes. Stir and serve. (This dish works well with cooked cabbage.)

Advanced

Generously season the chicken with Lawry's Seasoned Salt and black pepper; massage into the meat. Place the chicken in a large pot with the sliced onions. Cover the chicken well with mild curry powder and then use half that amount of the hot curry powder (curry stains your hands so use rubber gloves). Use two large, long metal spoons to mix the curry power and onions together. Let this mixture sit for an hour, then sprinkle in more mild and hot curry powder and mix again with the spoons.

Cover the bottom of a skillet with cooking oil and heat to very hot. Sprinkle in one handful of sugar. Sear the meat, remove it and return to the pot. Do not fry the onions.

Gravy

In another pot, add 3 large boxes of Swanson's Chicken Broth. Bring to a boil. Add ½ teaspoon crushed dried red peppers, a bay leaf, a dash of Worcestershire sauce and chicken bouillon to taste.

Once the broth starts to boil, start pouring in the Wondra flour. Continue to pour until the broth thickens like gravy. Stir constantly. Once desired texture is acquired, add the chicken and onions, and let everything simmer on medium-low heat for 1 hour. Stir every 10 to 15 minutes, and scrape the bottom of the pot because the flour sinks to the bottom and will burn if not stirred properly. Cook until the chicken is done. Serve with Coconut Rice.

 **MOM'S GERMAN CHOCOLATE CAKE**

You'll need two 9-inch cake pans
1 box Betty Crocker German Chocolate
    Cake with Pudding
1 can Carnation evaporated milk
1 c. sugar

1 stick butter
4 egg yolks
1 tsp. vanilla extract
1 c. chopped pecans
1½ c. coconut

Preheat oven: 350 degrees
Preparation time: 30 min.
Baking time: 25 to 30 min.

Beginners

Follow the instructions on the cake box. A good way to tell if the cake is done is to press lightly on the top of the cake with your fingertip. When the cake springs back and you can't see the indentation of your finger, it is done.

Filling/Frosting

Put 1 cup of sugar, 1 stick of butter, 1 teaspoon of vanilla and 4 egg yolks into a pot. (In order to separate the egg yolks from the egg whites, I wear rubber gloves and hold the cracked egg in my hand. The egg white slips through my fingers and I put the egg yolk in a bowl.) Mix well.

Heat this mixture on medium heat until it bubbles. It's important to stir constantly so the egg stays smooth and blended. Reduce the heat to low and continue to cook for 12 minutes. The mixture is going to thicken. Add the chopped pecans and coconut.

Let this filling cool before icing the cake with it. Use a knife to spread a ½-inch layer on the first cooled cake; stack the second cooled cake atop the first with the filling between them. Ice the top. When icing the sides, the icing may begin slipping. Put just a little on at a time. I put my cake in the freezer for 30 minutes when I have finished icing it to lock the icing in place.

Advanced

Bake the cake.

Put 1 cup sugar, 1 stick butter, 1 teaspoon vanilla and 4 egg yolks into a pot. Bring mixture to a bubble on medium heat, stirring constantly so the eggs stay smooth and blended. Lower the temperature to simmer and continue to cook for 12 minutes. The mixture is going to thicken. Add the chopped pecans and coconut. Let this filling cool before using it to fill the area between the first and second layers. Use the rest to ice the cake.

HOT ROLLS

Hot rolls freeze very well. This recipe yields 50 to 60 rolls, so they last a long time. I recommend you make these days before a big dinner and take them out of the freezer as needed. They take a while to fix, but they're well worth the trouble!

> 2 c. milk
> 1 c. sugar
> 3 packets Fleischmann's dry yeast
> 5 c. flour (Gold Medal All Purpose)
> 6 eggs
> 1 c. vegetable oil (Mazola)
>
> Preheat oven: 400 degrees
> Preparation time: 3 hours
> Baking time: 5 to 7 min.

Beginners

Making homemade bread by hand is quickly becoming a lost art. That makes it extra special! Your family and friends will love this bread. This is an easy recipe, so take courage and let's get started.

Stir 2 cups of milk and 1 cup of sugar into a pot and scald. (Scalding means that you almost bring it to a boil but not quite. You will see bubbles forming around the edges but not in the middle.) Turn the heat off and remove the pot from the burner.

Sift 5 cups flour. When you are measuring the flour it is important that you don't shake the flour down in the cup, or you'll end up with more flour than the recipe calls for. Instead use the flat side of a knife and scrape across the top of a full cup of flour. Put the flour in a sifter and sift it into a big bowl.

Fleischmann's yeast has 3 packages of yeast combined in 1 strip. It is found in the market next to the flour. When you add water to the yeast, if it's too hot or too cold the dough will not rise. A wise lady taught me how to make sure the temperature is right every time. Cut the end open on each packet of yeast and pour it into a bowl. Test the temperature of the water from the tap with your finger. It should be very warm to the touch. Put a small amount of that water in a cup and taste it. Even though it is warm to your touch it should only be lukewarm in your mouth. You would never want to drink anything that temperature— that's when it's perfect.

Add just enough water to the bowl to cover the yeast— about ½ cup—and immediately stir it with a fork until the yeast is dissolved.

In another bowl combine 6 eggs with 1 cup of oil and beat it with an electric mixer. Pour the milk mixture into the eggs and beat until completely mixed. Stick your finger in the mixture to make sure the milk has been cooled to a lukewarm temperature, then add the yeast and beat with the mixer until blended. Add the flour while mixing until everything is well blended.

Beginners and Advanced

Pour ¼ cup oil into a large bowl and spread the oil around on the sides and bottom. Pour in the dough and cover the bowl and bread dough with aluminum foil. Set it in a place that is free of drafts and that won't be disturbed while it's rising. Check the dough every ½ hour. The dough is ready when it reaches the top of the bowl.

Clear an area of your smooth counter or tabletop. Put 8 cups of flour (not sifted) in one pile. Melt 3 sticks of butter and put it into a bowl. You will also need 3 to 4 cookie sheets and a rolling pin.

Spread 2 cups of flour on the counter or table approximately 24 x 24 inches. Pour the dough into the center of the flour. *The goal is to use as little flour as possible to get the dough to a place where it can be rolled out without sticking to the rolling pin.* Starting at the farthest edge of the dough, begin working the flour into it. Keep moving the dough toward you while blending in the flour. When there is not enough flour under the dough to keep it from sticking to the surface, draw from the pile of flour on your side. You will probably use 4 to 5 cups of the flour.

Place the ball of dough away from you so that you can work on it a little at a time. Use a metal spatula to scrape the counter or table, and wash the excess dough off your hands. Sprinkle flour on your work area again, and this time take a large handful of the dough and place it in the center of the spread flour. Spread flour on the rolling pin and roll out the dough until it is ½ inch thick.

Use the top of a round glass to cut a circle in the dough. In order not to waste dough, try to cut the circles as close to each other as possible. Pick up the circle, dip it completely in butter, lifting it gently to allow the butter to drain, and place it on the cookie sheet, folding it in half. Place the folded rolls about ½ inch apart. Fill the cookie sheet and set them aside to rise. Do not cover the dough. It will take between 45 minutes and an hour for the rolls to rise; they should double in size.

Once the rolls rise, it's time to bake them. *The goal is for them to be light brown on both top and bottom.* Position the racks at the top and the bottom of your oven and place the cookie sheet on the bottom rack first, for 3 minutes or until the bottom is lightly brown. Then put them on the top rack for approximately 2 to 3 more minutes until the top of the rolls are lightly brown. Remember, that if you are planning to freeze these rolls, you will be heating them again so don't get them too brown.

Enjoy!

MACARONI AND CHEESE

At every mentoring fellowship class I host, Patrice White joins me. She volunteers her time to help me in many ways. The following is her recipe.

1 stick butter
2 bunches green onions
1 ½ tbsp. flour
2 cans evaporated milk (12 oz.)
1 pkg. pepper jack cheese (9 oz.)
2 beaten eggs
2 lbs. sharp cheddar cheese
1 16-oz. bag large elbow macaroni
Lawry's Seasoned Salt
salt
pepper
creole seasoning
cayenne pepper
2 jars sliced pimentos

Preheat oven: 350 degrees
Preparation time: 20 minutes
Baking time: 30 to 40 minutes

Beginners and Advanced
Cheese Sauce

Melt 1 stick of butter over low heat and sauté the green onions for 10 minutes. Add the flour and stir until dissolved—this will take approximately 10 minutes. Add the evaporated milk and beaten eggs and mix well. Add the grated pepper jack cheese and 1 pound of the grated sharp cheddar cheese, stirring often until cheese is melted completely. (Make sure it doesn't stick to the bottom of the pan.) Season to taste.

Prepare the macaroni according to the package instructions, drain and rinse.

Pour the cooked pasta into a casserole dish and mix in the pimentos. Pour the sauce over the macaroni and mix well. Top with the remaining 1 pound of cheddar cheese and dab with butter before putting it into the oven.

Bake at 350 degrees until cheese has thoroughly melted and the edges have browned—about 30 to 40 minutes. It's a good idea to check the oven after 25 minutes and continue cooking only as needed.

 **QUESADILLAS**

4 skinless and boneless chicken breasts
cumin
1 small jar of roasted red peppers
8 oz. pepper jack cheese
1 pkg. flour tortillas
butter

Preheat oven: 400 degrees
Preparation time: 20 min.
Baking time: 35 min.

Beginners

Place the chicken breasts in a casserole dish. Sprinkle cumin over the top (cumin is found in the seasonings section). Add ¼ cup of water and cover. Bake for 35 minutes or until done. Remove and let cool. Cut the cooked meat into strips.

Grate the pepper jack cheese. On one flour tortilla spread a handful of chicken down the center followed by a handful of cheese. Lay roasted peppers across the cheese and fold it in half (the cheese will melt and flow to the edges when it gets hot).

Melt 2 tablespoons of butter in a skillet. The skillet should be hot when you put the tortilla in. Brown the quesadilla on one side and then on the other. Use a metal spatula to press the tortilla flat before turning. Cut each quesadilla into four pieces and serve with salsa.

Advanced

Bake the chicken with cumin seasoning. Remove it from the heat. After it has cooled, cut it into strips. Grate the pepper jack cheese. On a flour tortilla spread a handful of chicken down the center, followed by a handful of cheese. Place roasted peppers across the cheese, then fold the tortilla in half.

Melt 2 tablespoons of butter in a skillet. The skillet should be hot when you put the tortilla in. Brown the quesadilla on one side and then on the other. Use a metal spatula to press the tortilla flat before turning it. Cut each quesadilla into four pieces and serve with salsa.

Personal Recipes

Title: _____

From: _____

Ingredients: _____ _____

_____ _____

_____ _____

_____ _____

_____ _____

Preparation time: _____

Cooking time: _____

Instructions: _____

_____

_____

_____

_____

_____

_____

_____

Personal Recipes

Title: _____

From: _____

Ingredients: _____ _____

_____ _____

_____ _____

_____ _____

_____ _____

Preparation time: _____

Cooking time: _____

Instructions: _____

_____

_____

_____

_____

_____

_____

_____

Personal Recipes

Title: _____

From: _____

Ingredients: _____   _____

_____   _____

_____   _____

_____   _____

_____   _____

Preparation time: _____

Cooking time: _____

Instructions: _____

_____

_____

_____

_____

_____

_____

_____

Personal Recipes

Title: _____

From: _____

Ingredients: _____ _____

_____ _____

_____ _____

_____ _____

_____ _____

Preparation time: _____

Cooking time: _____

Instructions: _____

_____

_____

_____

_____

_____

_____

_____

Personal Recipes

Title: _____

From: _____

Ingredients: _____ _____

_____ _____

_____ _____

_____ _____

_____ _____

Preparation time: _____

Cooking time: _____

Instructions: _____

_____

_____

_____

_____

_____

_____

_____

Personal
Recipes

Title: _____

From: _____

Ingredients: _____   _____

_____   _____

_____   _____

_____   _____

_____   _____

Preparation time: _____

Cooking time: _____

Instructions: _____

_____

_____

_____

_____

_____

_____

_____

Personal Recipes

Title: _____

From: _____

Ingredients: _____ _____

_____ _____

_____ _____

_____ _____

_____ _____

Preparation time: _____

Cooking time: _____

Instructions: _____

_____

_____

_____

_____

_____

_____

Personal Recipes

Title: _____

From: _____

Ingredients: _____   _____

_____   _____

_____   _____

_____   _____

_____   _____

Preparation time: _____

Cooking time: _____

Instructions: _____

_____

_____

_____

_____

_____

_____

_____

Personal Recipes

Title: _____

From: _____

Ingredients: _____ _____

_____ _____

_____ _____

_____ _____

_____ _____

Preparation time: _____

Cooking time: _____

Instructions: _____

_____

_____

_____

_____

_____

_____

_____

Personal Recipes

Title: _____

From: _____

Ingredients: _____   _____

_____   _____

_____   _____

_____   _____

_____   _____

Preparation time: _____

Cooking time: _____

Instructions: _____

_____

_____

_____

_____

_____

_____

_____

Personal Recipes

Title: _____

From: _____

Ingredients: _____ _____

_____ _____

_____ _____

_____ _____

_____ _____

Preparation time: _____

Cooking time: _____

Instructions: _____

_____

_____

_____

_____

_____

_____

Personal Recipes

Title: _____

From: _____

Ingredients: _____ _____

_____ _____

_____ _____

_____ _____

_____ _____

Preparation time: _____

Cooking time: _____

Instructions: _____

_____

_____

_____

_____

_____

_____

_____

Personal Recipes

Title: _____

From: _____

Ingredients: _____ _____

_____ _____

_____ _____

_____ _____

_____ _____

Preparation time: _____

Cooking time: _____

Instructions: _____

_____

_____

_____

_____

_____

_____

Index

For more information about Bunny Wilson's books, tapes, and speaking engagements, please contact: New Dawn Productions, P.O. Box 2601, Pasadena, CA 91102 or check out her website: www.frankandbunny.com